Praise for *The Kingdom*

"The move from a church-centric to a kingdom-centric perspect...
as profound as the shift from an earth-centric Ptolemaic universe to a
helio-centric Copernican universe. We need people who can help us re-
imagine our place in the grand scheme of things (the kingdom of God).
We need people who can help us language the thoughts that allow us
to live differently in light of the truth. Jeff has served us well on both
counts. This is a must-read for those who 'get it' and want to help others
'get it' too.

Reggie McNeal
Missional Leadership Specialist, Leadership Network

"Jeff Christopherson's *Kingdom Matrix* helps aspiring church planters
and practitioners get above the fads and trends of the moment to discover God's timeless plan for expanding His Kingdom. He effectively
argues that the mission of the church is rooted in the mission of God.
Churches that want to bear 'fruit that remains' will be very conscious of
these Kingdom principles and follow them carefully. I am grateful for this
book!"

JD Greear
Founder and Senior Pastor of Summit Church, Durham NC

"Jeff Christopherson is one of the brightest missional minds in North
America. In *The Kingdom Matrix,* he helps Christian leaders reconcile the
altruistic impulses that so many unchurched people possess, with the
hope of Christ that the church is uniquely positioned and commissioned
to deliver. This isn't just a book of theories, but tested applications
borne out of the context of his ministry."

Kevin Ezell
President, North American Mission Board

"When I first heard Jeff share his Kingdom Matrix I was spellbound. It's
an incredible book with eternal truth that can be applied to both people
and churches. He has a life that backs up the message and a ministry
that multiplies it as well. I highly encourage all the young pastors and
church planters I work with to read it slowly."

Bob Roberts Jr.
Founder and Senior Pastor of NorthWood Church in Keller, TX

"The most important thing about a book is its author. Jeff Christopherson is the real deal. He has successfully done what he writes about. He has excelled in a very difficult mission field. This book presents brilliant insights for church planters and all levels of church leadership. It is also paves the way for every disciple to better fulfill God's unique call on their lives. Digest this distilled wisdom from a kingdom veteran and pass it on to others."

John Worcester
Church Planting Specialist

"The Church needs to be awakened to the reality of the Kingdom of God—His global movement that will end around His throne with men and women from every tribe, tongue, people, and nation. There is no voice in contemporary culture that understands this more than Jeff Christopherson. I am so thankful for this book that speaks straight to the heart of this issue. May the awakening begin!"

Vance Pitman
Founder and Senior Pastor of Hope Church in Las Vegas

"Jeff Christopherson has a unique way of seeing things. I always enjoy talking with Jeff because he invariably offers a fresh, insightful perspective on issues that really matter. This book is his magnum opus. In it he will challenge and inspire you and compel you to live your life differently after you read it."

Richard Blackaby
President of Blackaby Ministries International

"Jeff's words flow from a life and ministry that qualify him to speak about Kingdom impact. These insights are focused through the lens of a practical missiologist and will challenge the heart and mind of every church leader—it sure challenged me!"

Al Gilbert
Executive Director of Love Loud, North American Mission Board

"If you are happy with a God, you can explain in a 20-minute sermon and a church you can influence with the size of your 'market share' and a life you can control with protective boundaries, don't read this book. You won't like it. You won't like the questions it will raise or the answers it gives. But if you have an itch in your soul that has not been scratched by what you see, hear, and experience in our self-absorbed evangelical culture, dive into this book and don't come up for air until God has turned your life upside-right."

Connie Cavanaugh
Speaker, Author of From Faking It to Finding Grace

"Several years ago I had the privilege of hearing Jeff Christopherson share *The Kingdom Matrix*. I remember thinking, 'This is incredibly profound; more people need to hear this message.' Thank you, Jeff, for not only sharing your insight with the rest of us, but for giving us such a Kingdom-focused example to follow through your own personal life and ministry. I believe this book will be a complete game changer for many who read it!"

Brian Bloye
Pastor and Founder of West Ridge Church, Atlanta GA

"I have been waiting too long for Jeff to get his concepts of the kingdom of God in book form. So have you—though you may not have known it. If we have any real hope of bringing the Good News of Jesus Christ into our world, our cities and communities, it must be from a kingdom perspective. Jesus didn't simply bring the gospel; he brought the gospel of the Kingdom. Helping us 'get this' is the gift Jeff Christopherson gives us in *The Kingdom Matrix*. This is not a 'read it once' book. You will want to keep it close by and wear it out."

Lance Ford
Author of Right Here Right Now *and* UnLeader

KINGDOM MATRIX

*designing a church for
the Kingdom of God*

JEFF CHRISTOPHERSON
FOREWORD BY ED STETZER

Published in Boise, Idaho by Russell Media
Web: http://www.russell-media.com

This book may be purchased in bulk for educational, business, ministry,
or promotional use.

For information please email info@russell-media.com.

ISBN (print): 978-1-937-498-139
ISBN (e-book): 978-1-937-498-146

Printed in the United States of America

Dedication

This book is dedicated to the memory of my father, who entered into the eternal presence of King Jesus the day following this manuscript's submission. The "dash" between his chiseled dates paints a vivid picture of what it looks like to live and die as a Kingdom Expander. For his example I am evermore grateful and accountable.

Allan Richard Christopherson
June 6, 1936—May 22, 2012

Acknowledgments

To my life-long sweetheart, Laura. Thank you for walking unhesitatingly and obediently in faith-step after faith-step toward our shared calling to the Kingdom. You are the perfect answer to my parent's prayers of faith so many years ago. I love you.

To David Nickerson, my friend and fellow limping dreamer—thank you for so generously using your gift to help clarify, codify and edify. Your contributions to these ideas are vast and unmistakable.

To Adam Miller, an encourager and friend—thank you for believing and pushing. I might have given up without your honest excitement.

To Mark Russell—thanks for taking the risk.

To Kingdom-hearted pastors, leaders and church planters—thank you for your sacrificial examples of Kingdom living. You are heroes and the very hope through which the Great News travels. All royalties of this book go directly back to multiply your selfless tribe by supporting Kingdom-expanding church planters.

TABLE OF CONTENTS

FOREWORD

The "Kingdom of God" sounds silly to the world. The idea of an invisible, infinite reality beyond what we can observe with our senses smacks of fairy tales and children's stories. The world mocks the Church who, throughout history, has heralded a kingdom that has both come in power and has not yet been fully revealed. To the world, we are like children, playing with our imaginary friends. And the devil is content to allow that impression to persist.

The Enlightenment seared an empirical worldview into the modern mindset, crippling our ability to perceive spiritual reality. Yet, the invisible, immeasurable kingdom Jesus announced flies in the face of empiricism, challenging finite man to stake his entire life on something he can neither see or touch. Only by faith, guided by God's Word, can we peer through veil of this life and see what God sees. It is not what we can touch—what we can feel—that is real; the Bible teaches of a war waged between a kingdom of darkness and a kingdom of light that is the ultimate reality our darkened minds fail to grasp.

Many of you will recall the movie *The Matrix*, which continues to define the sci-fi genre of motion pictures, decades after its debut. The protagonist, Thomas Anderson (or "Neo"), learns that he has been asleep, plugged-in to a computer program designed to control his perception of reality. The computer program (called the Matrix) causes humans to believe they are living normal lives (with normal jobs, normal families, etc.), though they are really alone, comatose in an apocalyptic wasteland. Only when they are unplugged from the Matrix—rescued by someone outside of the deception—are they able to perceive things as they really are.

Similarly, Jesus adjusts our perception of reality. Though we are, by nature, inclined to hold tightly to those things we can see, touch and feel, Jesus re-prioritizes our affections to align with those of the His invisible kingdom. We begin to see things as they really are. The Kingdom of God is no fairy tale. The fairy tale is the lie that we embrace as sons of Adam and daughters of Eve. We are born blind, unable to see the inaugurated kingdom of king Jesus.

Jeff Christopherson has written *Kingdom Matrix* to help tear the shroud away from our eyes. Sadly, even those of us in ministry feel the tension between the kingdom of the world and the Kingdom of God. We wrestle with ego, pride, false humility, jealousy, workaholism, and apathy. Though Jesus came to earth to initiate the kingdom, it is has not yet been fully realized. In the meantime, we struggle as insurgents in a hostile land, rebelling against the Rebellion.

The Bible doesn't contain every word that proceeded from the mouth of Jesus. But among His words recorded in the gospels, many were spent describing the Kingdom of God. The kingdom ought to, consequently, make a noticeable impact on our ministries. Jeff takes pains to describe what the kingdom is, and what it is not. Using the Kingdom Matrix, we begin to see the Church as it should be, a kingdom outpost.

I pray *Kingdom Matrix* will challenge us to filter our ministries, strategies, and methods through the Kingdom of God. Only then will we start to see the gospel as less of a fairy tale, and more of a reality.

Ed Stetzer
President, LifeWay Research

INTRODUCTION

The frustration level among hard-working Christian leaders is high.

Why, despite all of our advances in methodology, resourcing and infrastructure, is the church of Jesus Christ not gaining ground? Sure, we may now have more large churches than any other time in Christian history, but if you dig a little deeper you discover there are simply fewer people attending church today than before the church growth movement began discipling our leaders en masse thirty years ago. We are working hard. What is wrong?

And then there is the question of *influence*. Despite our ongoing efforts to galvanize evangelicals into a political force for good, where can we find evidence that will demonstrate any advancement in our effectiveness in pushing back the darkness? What some in our society would celebrate as progress, evangelicals mourn as lost ground. What is even more troubling is that we intuitively know that there is still much more ground to be lost. It is simply a question of time. We are working really hard. What is wrong?

And what about the *disciple*? Maybe that's the wrong descriptor. How about "church member" or "church attendee" or, perhaps, consumer? The disciple at present seems to be an increasingly difficult client to please. Fortunately, as church leaders, we instinctively understand the unwritten contract of today's disciple: provide much, expect little, and above all, remember who pays the bills. So, with our marching orders clearly articulated, we get about the hard work of keeping our constituents spiritually entertained and unchallenged by focusing the church squarely upon itself. Oh boy, are we working hard. What is wrong?

For good reason, the frustration level among Christian leaders is high. Instinctively, most of us understand that pushing harder and faster will not change the trajectory of where we are heading. We desire the right things. We have the right goal. We are willing to pay a high price. So, what is wrong?

Perhaps we are driving in exactly the wrong direction.

The *Kingdom Matrix* is a blueprint designed to clarify and reposition the church of Jesus Christ in its fitting place within the Kingdom of God. It is a spiritual journey of discovery as we analyze the spiritual sources that inspire our decisions and make choices that serve one singular end—the Kingdom of God.

A small beginning . . .

> *"The kingdom of heaven is like a grain of mustard seed that a man took and sowed in his field. It is the smallest of all seeds, but when it has grown it is larger than all the garden plants and becomes a tree, so that the birds of the air come and make nests in its branches."*—King Jesus (Matthew 13:31-32 ESV)

If anything is clear from Jesus' teaching, it is that the Kingdom of God is not at all complicated. In order to participate in the counterintuitive experience of the Kingdom of God, we must simply, yet wholeheartedly, trust that the entire realm is dependent upon a lone Sovereign God. This King has no need for the business that I can deliver, nor is it held hostage to the proper execution of the most brilliant strategic thinking that I can muster. He requires only one simple course of action, Obedience. That action happens to be the only fitting response of a subject to his Sovereign.

Affronting, as it might seem to all the clever inventions of man, Jesus asks only for our allegiance. In that humbling weakness, He assumes the entire responsibility for His Kingdom plans, and does what He wishes with our mustard seed of faith. God takes that insignificant seed and carefully places it in the fertile soil of His providential desire. Taking on Himself the task of master planner, God creates the most intricate garden that has His image of eternity as its blueprint. From our fallen stations on earth, we seldom have eyes to see the wonders that God performs with our tiny mustard seed. That humbling and astounding revelation awaits the Christ-follower in heaven. But from time to time, God's grace allows us to take a little peek. These are amazing moments.

Let me share a very personal story that illustrates this great truth.

My parents, Allan and Helen Christopherson, were married on June 4, 1960 in Prince Albert, Saskatchewan, Canada. They soon began a family with the birth of their first child, a little blonde haired and blue-eyed girl, named Cathy. Three years after that, I was the second and final child to be added to their young family.

My father possessed an eighth grade education so his workplace options were very limited. He found work as a laborer cleaning beer storage tanks at Molson's brewery, which paid enough to support his young family. His salary package included only one benefit: free beer. The trajectory of my dad's life, similar to his colleagues, was not at all promising. Alcoholism had shipwrecked the lives of many, many men and their families at the brewery.

One weekend evening in 1967, my parents decided to go on a date. They telephoned a neighbor to babysit, gave her final instructions, jumped into their black 1958 VW Beetle, and headed to the old majestic Orpheum Theatre to take in a movie. Somewhere along the way, their interest was piqued to take in a religious movie called, *The Restless Ones*. Popcorn in hand they settled in to enjoy the entertainment that their $1.20 had purchased.

As a good movie should, the plot soon captured their attention and they found themselves engrossed in the human struggle illuminated in front of them. What my parents had not expected was a far more personal struggle that began to surface in their spirits. While watching the spiritual journey being represented on the silver screen, they found themselves being confronted with their personal sin and a desperate need for a great Savior.

While the actors on screen sat in a Chevy convertible, top down, listening to Billy Graham's preaching emanating through their radio, my parents fell under the deep conviction of the Holy Spirit. While the actors bowed their heads and prayed to receive Jesus Christ, my dad reached over and clasped my mom's hand, and together, they wrestled under the heavy conviction of the Living Christ. Something very serious was taking place in their hearts.

The movie soon reached its fitting conclusion, but to my parents' surprise, the evening was not yet over. A middle-aged man, dressed in a suit and tie, walked out to center stage and began to address the audience. He instructed that if anyone wished to respond to Christ, that they could get up from where they were seated, walk down the theater aisle, and come pray with him in the front of the theater. My parents surveyed the audience and didn't see anyone moving forward. The man patiently waited at the front for several minutes and then very politely thanked the audience for coming out.

My parents got out of their seats and made their way back to their old black VW. But something very new was happening. In the safety of closed sheet metal doors and the comfort of vinyl bucket seats, my parents began to talk about the implications of the commitments that they were contemplating. On that evening, in a parking lot outside the old Orpheum Theatre, Allan and Helen Christopherson surrendered their past, their present and their future to the saving power of Jesus Christ. They had been forever changed.

From that moment forward, life became an adventure. God led my father on a series of immediate faith steps that started with quitting his job at Molson's brewery, learning a new trade (welding), and eventually leading him to befriend a quiet yet spiritually intense man that God would use to forever change our family.

Jack Conner was a church-planting, faith-walking man of God who loved Jesus so recklessly that following Him seemed to always mean many personal inconveniences. He had already left the comfortable safety of a large church in Fresno, California, that he had previously established, to begin once again—this time in Prince Albert, Saskatchewan. When he and my dad first seren-dipitously met, my dad knew at once that he had found a kindred spirit. Jack was a man whose love for Jesus was obvious in every category of his life.

Yet Pastor Conner, as a church planter, had one major blind spot of which his new congregation soon became well aware. You see, he didn't think like a businessman. He really didn't even think like a normal man. To some, he actually thought like a madman. He had some quiet, inner compulsion that drove him to make one non-strategic move after the next. Instead of fine-tuning the systems and processes in the new church, he instead focused the attentions of his leaders outward. He expected barbers and carpenters and schoolteachers and accountants and welders to be involved in bringing the Good News to places where there was little to celebrate. Soon, new churches were dotting the map of towns, villages and native (First Nations) reservations all over the north. The Kingdom of God was moving forward.

When you enrolled in Pastor Conner's discipleship at Scarborough Baptist Church, you were signing up for a very problematic church experience. It was a costly discipleship. Many who visited would soon look for a more "full-service" church that was designed to be in tune to their needs. But those who stayed received a spiritual education that would transform the way that they would see everything. We didn't know it at the time—I am not even sure that Jack knew it, but he was building leaders for a nation.

God's gracious hand led my parents and their new faith to jump in the middle of a Kingdom-focused culture. This became the new normal for us. It was a gift.

Fast forward thirty-five years . . .

My father was invited to be on an interdenominational leadership team that would organize and host a Franklin Graham Crusade that was to take place in Saskatoon, Saskatchewan. One of the first organizing meetings was held in a large room where Christian leaders from all walks of life gathered for inspiration and instruction. My dad found his place at a round table and settled in to take in the evening. His spirit was both excited and grateful to be a part of this opportunity.

The chairman of the initiative walked up to the microphone, made some introductory comments, and then made a request of the audience, "I would like us to spend our first few moments celebrating what God has already done through the ministry of the Grahams. Would two or three of you in this room want to come to the microphone and share how the ministry of Billy Graham has impacted your life?"

My dad's heart began to race. He sensed the Holy Spirit saying, "Share your story." Yet his flesh said, "Speaking in front of a group this large? You're just a welder!" Before he knew it, he found himself taking shaky steps toward the microphone. He told the audience about that day in 1967 where he took his wife to *The Restless Ones* at the Orpheum Theatre in Prince Albert. He told the group about a skipped alter-call and an encounter with Christ in a VW Beetle. He told them about the church that they had found, and the adventure they continue to be on. He told them about those two small children who were being babysat by the neighbor were now spending their lives starting new churches all over Toronto, Ontario and across Chile in South America. "I do not know how many hundreds of lives are now in the Kingdom because my wife and I went to the movies that day."

While my father found his seat at his table, there seemed to be a holy hush settling in the room. An elderly man slowly made his way in a straight line to my dad. Tears flowing down his cheeks, he stammered as he introduced himself. "Hello, Allan, my name is Tom. Tom Dice. I am a retired family counselor in the area. I want you to know something, Allan. God asked me to bring that movie to Prince Albert. I rallied my friends and colleagues and we really expected great things to happen. Night after night we played the movie and night after night I stood before the audience and asked them to respond to Christ. Night after night I went home very disappointed. Until this day, to my knowledge, nobody ever responded. I thought my project was a failure. I wondered if I had heard God right in the first place. But I did hear Him, Allan. Now I see that it wasn't a failure." With joyful tears running down Tom's face, he embraced my dad and said, "Now I see. Praise Jesus, now I see . . ."

When we recall stories such as these, our spirit immediately identifies the Hero. Neither Tom Dice, nor Jack Conner nor my parents were the central figure orchestrating the events that culminated in this strategic win. Each was simply investing their mustard seed as the Master Planner nudged their hearts. Each had a simple part to play. The eternal garden was being planned and cultivated by an all-seeing Designer who merely asked one question: "Will you trust Me?"

We answer that question every day by what we do with a very small seed.

SECTION I

Deconstructing Christian Mythology

In order to turn around, first we must understand the direction we are going. There are three ways in which the contemporary evangelical church may be heading, en masse, in exactly the wrong direction. For many, these Kingdom assumptions have not been clearly understood, and, therefore, are not practiced.

These Kingdom assumptions relate directly to three myths that many have swallowed, hook, line and sinker. I have described these as:

The Myth of the Third Kingdom
The Myth of Church Growth
The Myth of Kingdom Turf

By recalibrating our thinking in these three areas, and then setting out to design a new church, or perhaps, re-engineer an existing congregation toward the priorities of Christ's Kingdom, we will see patterns and priorities that might be radically unfamiliar to the "normal" which we've known.

CHAPTER 1

THE MYTH OF THE THIRD KINGDOM
The Assumption of Sides

At any given moment I am either expanding the
Kingdom of God or the Dominion of Darkness. Period.

Sometimes the greatest insights we have come not from rational deductions, but from God's quiet whisper of instruction.

Let me share of one of those times.

I was speaking at a men's retreat of our church. The setting was a picturesque camp situated in the Muskoka country of northern Ontario. It was a cool, crisp fall evening with a gathering of men enjoying the camaraderie of brothers—most in honest anticipation of spiritual renewal.

Fellowship was intense and deep. Worship was heartfelt and robust. Testimonies revealed transparency, authenticity and brokenness. God was on the move.

The message I sensed God was asking me to deliver was simple: the calling of Christ is a calling of loyalty and courage. Jesus said, *"From the days of John the Baptist until now, the Kingdom of heaven has been forcefully advancing, and forceful men lay hold of it,"* (Matthew 11:12). God's call was a courageous call of loyalty and allegiance to a singular Sovereign King.

There was a quietness in the room; no one was looking at his watch, there was no shuffling or throat clearing—there was a sense of God's presence. And then something strange happened. It wouldn't have seemed strange to the hearers, but in my spirit I knew that something significant had just transpired. I made a simple statement, "There are only two spiritual realms—the Kingdom of God and the Dominion of Darkness. There isn't a third Kingdom. Every decision we make is inspired by, and advances the agenda of one of those two Kingdoms. There is no neutral territory."

The strangeness was, that as the words were coming from my mouth, I thought, "Hmm, that's right—I'd never thought of that before." God had shown something to me, which may have been painfully obvious to every other Christ-follower, but somehow had always eluded my grasp.

Looking back, I had always seen life in extremes. On one extreme, I knew of the Kingdom of God, and I knew that on occasion I participated in it. Instances where I may have given sacrificially to meet a need. Times when I had taken some major steps of faith because I had no doubt in God's leading. Really spiritual stuff.

Yet, on the other extreme, I knew of the Kingdom of Darkness—and yes, even as a pastor, I knew that at times I participated in its advancement as well. A careless word that offended someone deeply. A season of resentment toward a colleague. Lingering thoughts that were anything but pure. Really destructive stuff.

My two extremes were well established in my instinctive understanding—the selfless realm of the Kingdom of God, and the self-absorbed territory of the Dominion of Darkness. But in between these two Kingdom extremes existed a third mythical Kingdom—a much more ordinary realm. A grey territory that would contain the bulk of my time and energy. Not good. Not evil. Just life. "The Kingdom of the Spiritually Insignificant" may have been the designation I would have given it.

The problem with the Third Kingdom is that it doesn't actually exist.

		KINGDOM SOURCE	
		DOMINION OF DARKNESS	KINGDOM OF GOD
FORM	SACRED		
	SECULAR		

IS EVERYTHING BLACK OR WHITE?

As I have reflected upon God's Word from the insight of that day, I have observed that belief in the existence of this middle, grey Kingdom is really just lethargic spiritual discernment—spiritual apathy which usually ends in spiritual frustration and defeat. Why does God urge us to "pray continually" (1 Thes. 5:17)? Maybe the decisions we make in the normalcy of living are of spiritual significance. Perhaps the space the bulk of our lives occupies actually matters in the spiritual realm.

Maybe it matters a lot.

What did Jesus mean when he spoke of both light and darkness in the life of a person? Where is the grey of the insignificant? Why did he follow up the light/darkness theme with a divine observation that we can only serve one of two masters?

The eye is the lamp of the body. If your eyes are good, your whole body will be full of light. But if your eyes are bad, your whole body will be full of darkness. If then the light within you is darkness, how great is that darkness! No one can serve two masters. Either he will hate the one and love the other, or he will be devoted to the

one and despise the other. You cannot serve both God and Money.
(Matthew 6:22-24)

The masters to whom we pay allegiance
clearly indicate the Kingdom we advance at
any given moment. In the battle of good and
evil, there clearly is no demilitarized zone.
We are for Him or we are against Him.
We are never undecided.

Undoubtedly, Jesus wanted his followers to grasp the significance of the Kingdoms that we occupy. Everything is light and darkness. Just because I claim to be a reborn child of God does not mean that I automatically advance the Kingdom of God. Just because my church claims to be a community of Christ does not automatically mean that it is advancing the cause of Christ. I was discovering that the Kingdom of God advances only through the counter-cultural faith steps of allegiance to the King. The masters to whom we pay allegiance clearly indicate the Kingdom we advance at any given moment. In the battle of good and evil, there clearly is no demilitarized zone. We are for Him or we are against Him. We are never undecided.

Every decision that I make as an individual and every decision that a church makes corporately is actually a spiritual decision. Spiritual forces inspire us to pursue one of two paths. These are not equal spiritual forces, but they are exclusive in the direction that they're moving. Darkness persuades us to save ourselves by serving ourselves—even if only for a season—wink, wink. Light calls us to faith. It reminds us of the essence of our relationship with God and inspires us to continue walking in the manner in which we began this relationship. Consolidation, even for a season, is a term without faith, and therefore a season of dark spiritual disconnection.

And so we scratch our heads and ask, "Why does Jesus have to always be this 'all or nothing' God? What harm can come from a little grey?"

That is a really good question.

DELUSIONS OF THE THIRD KIND

Belief in this Third Kingdom creates a delusional brand of spirituality, one of rationalization and self-justification. This mythical Kingdom has been pursued by some of the godliest men of faith our world has known—only to their own spiritual mortification.

Take the great father of faith for example. Abraham, the man who spent a lifetime advancing God's Kingdom through faith step after incredible faith step, from time to time, backtracked from his advance. Genesis 20 documents some of the delusional thought processes that occur when we relegate areas of our lives to the category of "spiritually insignificant."

Abraham, on his faith journey, was faced with a spiritual decision that at its very heart asked the question, "Do I trust God?" Abraham was blessed with a very beautiful wife. Apparently Sarah turned a lot of heads in her day. As Abraham would encounter new people, his heart must have swelled with joy as he would hear the comments from others as to what a lucky man he was. But, as Dr. Hook sang, it's not all fun and games being in Abraham's position. *"When you're in love with a beautiful woman you know it's hard. Everybody wants her, everybody loves her. Everybody wants to take your baby home . . ."* Abraham foresaw dangers ahead from having such a beautiful wife. "I must be proactive," he must have thought. "I'll reposition reality ever so slightly so that I can side-step some upcoming landmines."

DELUSION #1: TRUTH IS FLEXIBLE.

And so Abraham came up with a reasonable plan. "I'll pass my wife off as my sister! No one will harm me for having a beautiful sister—in fact they may bless me! This is a win-win proposition. I'm safe. I may even be blessed. And what is beautiful about this is that it's not totally a lie; Sarah is my half-sister. We'll just keep quiet about the wife part."

Can you imagine how honored Sarah must have felt about her husband's scheme of being flexible with truth? I wonder how valued she felt when she was reduced to becoming a token of safe passage for her husband when Abraham handed her over to the pagan king Abimelech.

Now Abraham moved on from there into the region of the Negev and lived between Kadesh and Shur. For a while he stayed in Gerar, and there Abraham said of his wife Sarah, 'She is my sister.' Then Abimelech king of Gerar sent for Sarah and took her. (Genesis 20:1-2)

When the words that I speak are true,
no matter how difficult they may be, the
Kingdom of God is forcefully advanced

When I live in the delusional space of the Third Kingdom, truth becomes flexible. It was true that Sarah was Abraham's half-sister, but the fact that she was also his wife trumped any validity to his "sister" claim. Even when he was confronted with his lie, Abraham unapologetically clung to his flexible truth strategy.

She really is my sister, the daughter of my father though not of my mother; and she became my wife. And when God had me wander from my father's household, I said to her, 'This is how you can show

your love to me: Everywhere we go, say of me, "He is my brother."
(Genesis 20:12-13)

The myth of the Third Kingdom introduces a new fictitious grey zone to the idea of truth. This grey zone may seem innocent enough when we relegate it to the spiritual category of "insignificant." But when the words that we speak are half-truths, there is always only one result: the Kingdom of Darkness is extended through my rationalization. However, when the words that I speak are true, no matter how difficult they may be, the Kingdom of God is forcefully advanced.

DELUSION #2: I AM SPECIAL.

In order to rationalize a half-truth (which of course is a full lie), I must establish an end that justifies these dubious means. For those of us who would consider ourselves a part of the family of God, this is not a difficult assignment. All that we have to do is look around and see the crumbling ethical foundations of our land, and in a sense of moral righteousness, we can justify almost any action as being preferable to the alternative—the growing godlessness of our culture. After all, we are on the side of God. We are his special people. God needs our action!

This second delusion presupposes two themes of arrogance. First, God needs me. God is unable to accomplish his purposes apart from me. My life, my church, even my denomination is so essential to the work of God, that He would be hamstrung without our efforts on His behalf. And second, because I am so special and essential, God is incapable and/or unwilling to speak to or work through anyone else. The thought of it seems preposterous to us.

"Why would He even want to?"

Christian occupation of the mythical territory of the Third Kingdom requires incredible arrogance on the part the church. This arrogance originates with the assumption that our pragmatic means to Kingdom expansion are preferable to God over the actions of a Kingdom-Seeker (a term more fully defined later) who, outside of a relationship with God, values and lives the principles of the Kingdom of God.

Abraham was under such a delusion:

I said to myself, 'There is surely no fear of God in this place.' (Genesis 20:11)

Abraham knew that he was special. He was. He couldn't escape it. He had a relationship with God that was unlike anyone else's—he was called "God's friend." It would seem to be impossible to be more special than that. The problem is, when it comes to advancing spiritual Kingdoms, status is not essential; it's just greatly beneficial. The Kingdom of God is built through one simple method: the King reveals His course of action and we subjugate ourselves to His will by cooperating with His revelation.

As unfortunate as it may seem to those
of us who claim status in His Kingdom,
God seems persistently unwilling to limit
His influence to the chosen few.

Abraham, a man with elevated spiritual status, made a wide-sweeping generalization and, from it, drew some significant and dangerous conclusions. Abraham's belief was that there was *no fear of God* in the land of King Abimelech. From that belief, and from the certainty of his own status as special—Abraham easily justified his minor indiscretion. What difference will one white lie make in the face of such ungodliness?

This would make sense if the Kingdom of God were limited to me and mine. But as unfortunate as it may seem to those of us who claim status in His Kingdom, God seems persistently unwilling to limit His influence to the chosen few. We may take great pride in our spiritual status—but God works through those who do not. Abraham, a man with status, makes a choice of disobedience, which advances the Kingdom of Darkness. Abimelech, a man with no spiritual standing, is blessed to hear the revelation of God.

> *But God came to Abimelech in a dream one night and said to him, 'You are as good as dead because of the woman you have taken; she is a married woman.'* (Genesis 20:3)

God speaks to pagan kings? God reveals his will to outsiders? Why didn't God go directly to the one with covenantal status?

It's probably safe to say that He did.

This was an area of consistent disobedience by Abraham—this wasn't his first occasion of lying and trading his wife's honor for his own security. This wasn't even the first time he had been caught in his lie. This was an area of Abraham's life that was clearly slotted in the mythical Third Kingdom. And so the Kingdom of God had to be advanced apart from those with status.

When I read passages of Scripture like this, I'm always amazed by the correlation between the advancement of God's Kingdom and the power of God's grace. Abraham sinned. Sarah was used. Abimelech was duped. God was sovereign.

> *Then God said to him in the dream, 'Yes, I know you did this with a clear conscience, and so I have kept you from sinning against me. That is why I did not let you touch her.'* (Genesis 20:6)

Abimelech, the pagan king, was not the great outsider as the one with standing presupposed. Although he may not have had Abraham's position, he experienced a great measure of God's grace. The myth of the Third Kingdom flourishes as long as the church of Jesus Christ prefers to see itself as the singular object of God's grace rather than an agent of God's grace.

We'll talk more about this later, too.

DELUSION #3: MY SIN'S INFLUENCE IS NEGLIGIBLE.

The impact of the Kingdom of Darkness, we all understand. Two hijacked jet planes steered straight into two populated office towers. The effect of that dark decision is obvious to all. The sinister masterminds accounted for some of it—but even they were shocked by the results of their actions. The outcome was far greater than they had hoped. Instead of their planned two gaping holes of terror, they brought total annihilation to the symbols they hated so deeply.

We get that. The Kingdom of Darkness produces attitudes of darkness, which in turn generate the plans of darkness to further expand the territory of darkness. A sadistic cycle we've seen over and over again throughout history. Understood. Evil produces increased evil. Darkness produces darkness.

If the Kingdom of Darkness produces darkness, what then does the middle-mythical Third Kingdom produce?

A delusion of inconsequence.

Abraham, being the man of God that he was, wouldn't have pursued his fraudulent course of action had he known the devastating affects his sin would unleash on a king and his kingdom. Abraham was convinced that his "half-sin" would have no harmful result of significance—so he continued in his sin.

The irony of this shouldn't escape us. Abraham was chosen by God to be a blessing to the nations. Instead, straight out of the gate, Abraham, because of this enormous spiritual blind spot in his life, becomes not a blessing but a curse to the nations. Ouch. Abimelech (the pagan king) confronts Abraham (the friend of God) about his unscrupulous behavior and the guilt it has brought upon his kingdom.

Then Abimelech called Abraham in and said, 'What have you done to us? How have I wronged you that you have brought such great guilt upon me and my Kingdom? You have done things to me that should not be done.' (Genesis 20:9)

Things that seemed an innocent shade of grey to Abraham appeared terrifyingly dark to Abimelech. It all depended on which side of the consequences you lived. Abraham couldn't imagine consequences being a reality of life in the Third Kingdom. Abimelech couldn't imagine that a prophet (the first time the word prophet was used in the Bible it was spoken by God to Abimelech) of God could intentionally cause such pain and calamity in his life, in his family and in his Kingdom.

God healed Abimelech, his wife and his slave girls so they could have children again, for the LORD had closed up every womb in Abimelech's household because of Abraham's wife Sarah. (Genesis 20:17-18)

The myth of the Third Kingdom forces a middle grey over the clear distinction of darkness and light. As we'll see in Jesus' teaching, that middle grey is far more insidious than darkness, and yet, unfortunately, far more palatable to God's people.

DELUSION #4: MY REPENTANCE IS SUPERFICIAL.

I have a friend named Ken. Ken was an Olympic athlete in training when I met him and was probably one of the most disciplined people I had ever met. He had already won a bronze medal and had his sights set on gold. Everything in his life was harnessed and directed toward accomplishing this goal.

Ken wasn't always like this. There was a major portion of Ken's young adult life where he had two incongruent pursuits: his sport and a self-destructive need to prove that he was tough. Ken was a wild man. The pictures tattooed on his arms and back told a lot of his story—in and out of trouble with the law, living life on and then well over the edge, concentrating on his sport and then getting sidelined because of his private life. Ken's life was out of control.

But then something happened. Ken went to visit his brother whose accommodations were supplied courtesy of a federal penitentiary. His brother was a hard man who influenced much of the course of Ken's life. Recently, Ken began to receive letters from his brother, telling him about how he had changed—about the forgiveness he had experienced in a relationship with Jesus Christ. Letter after letter encouraged Ken to change his life's course and receive Jesus to fill that empty place he had been filling with hard living. It was inconceivable to Ken that his brother could have changed or that there could be any hope for his own life.

After visiting the penitentiary, Ken climbed into his van and drove down the quiet rural highway. He could not believe what he had just experienced. This angry, tense, flippant, older brother was changed completely. There in his place in that visiting room was a peaceful, calm, caring brother who was concerned about his younger brother's welfare. What could account for this change? As he drove down the road, tears began to well up in his eyes— soon he had to pull over because he was weeping uncontrollably. In the driver's seat of that van, pulled over on the side of the road, Ken made his peace with God.

A couple of years later, our small group Bible study decided to meet outside on a beautiful summer's evening. We met at a park around a couple of wooden picnic tables next to the cold and clear mountain-fed waters of the Bow River. An interested young woman asked Ken, "Are you ever tempted to go back to that old life?" I'll never forget Ken's response, because it so vividly paints the picture of true repentance.

Ken replied, "Imagine you had been drowning in that river. Imagine that you were calling and calling for help and no one came. Imagine that you called one last time, reached out for help, and still nobody came. You gave up all hope and just began to sink to the bottom. And then you heard a splash. Someone was diving into that river and pulling you out. He gave you some warm, dry clothes and a blanket. He saved you from that river."

And then Ken looked up and said, "If you had experienced that, how would you feel about that river? Would you want to get close to it? Would you want to put on a bathing suit and splash around on the edge? No. You wouldn't want to go near it because you see it differently than anyone else. It tried to kill you." Ken looked at the river again and said, "That is how I see my old life. I never want to be there again."

The picture that Ken painted is the perfect picture of repentance. Two little Greek words *'meta'* (change) and *'noeo'* (mind) sandwiched together as a bold declaration of a transformed life. No dabbling around the edges of darkness. It is a resolute decision to walk in the light.

For repentance to be sincere, light and darkness must be unambiguous. This is not a climate friendly to the Third Kingdom, which thrives on the indistinctness of a blurry grey mediocrity.

Let's revisit Abraham and Abimelech. Abraham was brought before the king and evidence was abundant that he had lied about Sarah. What was Abraham's reaction? Brokenness and genuine repentance? No. Instead he offered a lawyerly attempt of rationalizing his decision.

> *Abimelech asked Abraham, "What was your reason for doing this?" Abraham replied, "I said to myself, 'There is surely no fear of God in this place, and they will kill me because of my wife.' Besides, she really is my sister . . ."* (Genesis 20:10-12)

Abraham's defense in summary: "You're a pagan . . . I was afraid . . . and technically, it wasn't a total lie." The spiritual outsider was experiencing the full consequences of Abraham's sin. What was the prophet's response? Verbal gymnastics to admit no wrong doing, all the while further entrenching his claim as distinct and superior from those who have no spiritual standing. The myth of the Third Kingdom was well intact in Abraham's life.

Although genuine repentance is not a language spoken in the Third Kingdom, it can be heard in other realms. Abimelech the pagan spoke this heavenly language like it was his mother tongue.

Then Abimelech brought sheep and cattle and male and female slaves and gave them to Abraham, and he returned Sarah his wife to him. And Abimelech said, 'My land is before you; live wherever you like.' To Sarah he said, 'I am giving your brother a thousand shekels of silver. This is to cover the offense against you before all who are with you; you are completely vindicated.' (Genesis 20:14-16)

Notice the staggering contrast. Abraham attempted to cover up his sin with carefully chosen words. Abimelech covered Abraham's transgression with a choice to self-sacrifice. Abraham was concerned with his own security over Sarah's honor. Abimelech was concerned with Sarah's reputation over his own securities. Abraham considered himself a God-fearer and considered Abimelech his spiritual inferior. Abimelech demonstrated his fear of God by his actions, and at least in this encounter, established that true spirituality is not found in his position, but in the humility and honesty of his worship.

For those of us who claim status, this should be a deeply troubling concept.

GREY IS THE NEW BLACK.

Every fall the fashion industry revs up the marketing machine to convince us to replace our tired frumpy wardrobe with all of its exciting new styles and colors. The jingle is always very familiar, every year a new sense of *deja vu*. The fall that I write this, Laura, my wife tells me that this year's installment is, brown is the new black. Black has been the standard and seems to have held up over the years. But now it's out. Brown is in. Brown? Who are they kidding?

We have a new black in our Christian culture. It's less exciting than brown. Much less. It's dreary, ambiguous, ill-defined grey. As we've seen illustrated in the life of Abraham, grey can be as dark as black. Perhaps much darker.

And so, we have two Kingdoms, no more. Two spiritual realms. If we want more options than that, we close our Bibles, and open the wondrous fable of the Third Kingdom. This Kingdom is less demanding. But less honest, too. Had you ever wondered why Jesus preferred cold to lukewarm?

I know your deeds, that you are neither cold nor hot. I wish you were either one or the other! So, because you are lukewarm—neither hot nor cold—I am about to spit you out of my mouth. (Revelation 3:15)

Cold has chosen its side. Lukewarm is playing it from both ends. Lukewarm is keeping its options opened. Lukewarm has less integrity than cold. Lukewarm mocks God by thinking that its one foot in each world somehow goes unnoticed by the Omniscient One.

Grey is black, only more so. Participation in the Kingdom of God demands clear thinking and clear decisions of allegiance.

CHAPTER 2

THE MYTH OF CHURCH GROWTH
The Assumption of Lost Ground

It is possible to participate in church expansion and unintentionally be an agent for shrinking the Kingdom of God.

Kingdom leadership isn't usually easy. Sometimes it is incredibly difficult. Often it is one person standing alone, resolutely determined to resist the baser demands of others in order to accomplish something with eternal significance. This kind of leadership looks beyond self-interest toward something greater—often at a great personal cost.

These are the kinds of leaders that a lost world is waiting desperately to find: people who will look at the church in a different way—not as "the goal," but instead, as "the vehicle" to the goal.

What is the difference?

Let me illustrate it this way. I was recently referred to the website of a very prominent church where I found some disturbing words penned proudly by their pastor and boldly displayed on their front page. Without blushing, this pastor composed the following sentiment:

> *As I look around our great city, I can see spectacular buildings dedicated to commerce, culture and government—some are new, some are restored, and all are intended to stand for generations. The Kingdom of God needs a home to equal them.*

What was implied, if not explicitly stated, by this pastor is that he saw his church and the Kingdom of God as one and the same. It was a new spiritual realm that needed a home so as not to be dwarfed by worldly temples of commerce and government. The argument seems to go like this: a multi-million dollar investment in remodeling facilities was, in fact, preparing a home for the very Kingdom of God. The church, therefore, is the unrivaled goal; the Kingdom is . . . well, the church. The edifice was what contained the realm of God's rule—His Kingdom. Interesting theology to be sure. But, unfortunately, this is not as uncommon as you might think.

Many of us are just a little subtler in masking our aspirations.

I recall observing a study from a major European news source that had, as its hypothesis, *Christianity makes no net positive contribution to society.*

To prove their assumption, the Europeans rolled their investigative team into a major urban city in the southern United States and began to count things. For those who had ears to hear, the Europeans had some truth to tell.

They started counting churches. My tribe was well represented. Baptist this, that, or something else dominated many strategic intersections. Methodists, Assemblies of God, Catholics, Presbyterians, Anglicans and, of course, those non-denominational churches were in abundance. Churches of all shapes, sizes, styles and colors were listed in their ledger. It was a very, very long list.

They chose this particular city because it was thought to have the highest church-to-population ratio of any major urban center on the planet. Certainly a city like this with such exposure to a Gospel witness must have a transforming influence on its residents. Unquestionably a city like this, which has produced such a disproportionate number of Christian spokesmen, who have a global ministry, should also have had a dramatic impact at home. Surely a city like this, which houses some of North America's largest churches complete with a plethora of niche ministries carefully crafted to meet every subtle nuance of spiritual need, should have a dramatic affect on the adjacent neighborhoods it gobbles up.

But there were more things to count. They strapped on their Birkenstocks, un-holstered their slide-rules and started counting problems: suicides, drug/alcohol addiction, teen-age pregnancies, homelessness, sexual crimes, murders, child abuse. The kinds of problems that seem to have no easy answer.

You know where this is going, don't you? The Europeans un-packed their calculators and began to do the math. In every cat-egory of social verve, this very churched city bumped along the very bottom as compared to similar sized cities throughout the world. In subsequent interviews with leading pastors in that city to unveil their findings, the common refrain from these men of God was, "That's not necessarily my responsibility; my job is to shepherd my flock."*

"How many are you running?" (or, "How many have you benched?")

I am a goal-oriented guy. Give me a numerical goal worth pursuing and I'll focus all my energy toward it. Goals give me a buzz. I know there is psychological help available for me, but for now I am going to enjoy being off-balanced.

Goal lovers have something in common: we love the mantra, "Those who fear numbers usually have none to report." Gotcha! How do you get out of that one? If that's not enough, we go on and become deeply theological: "You don't think God loves num-bers? He loves them so much that He named the fourth book of the Bible after them!" Wham! What can you say to that stel-

---

*I have intentionally chosen to mask the identity of the city in this study for the purpose of universal effect. The ratios are not dramatically different among many highly churched communities in North America. Conversely, new studies show a dramatic impact of social reform where higher church ratios exist in many regions experiencing new and rapid ex-pansion, ex. Southeast Asia.

lar line of theological reasoning? Yet sometimes there remains a stubborn few who still look at us goal-oriented people with a slight air of skepticism. Unimaginable! For those who still are not yet fully convinced, we bring out the big guns. To do this, we must lower our voices, cast our glance downward and say in the most spiritually-sounding tone we can muster, "But sister, every number represents a soul that God loves." Shut the book. Case closed. We have yet again validated, beyond a reasonable doubt, our neurosis with numbers.

> You gather a group of us in a room, hit the
> timing feature on your digital watch, and
> start counting the seconds until the first
> conversation goes the way of, "so,
> how many are you running these days?"

Most pastors wouldn't want to confess this, but sometimes we can be a pretty ungodly bunch. You gather a group of us in a room, hit the timing feature on your digital watch, and start counting the seconds until the first conversation goes the way of, "So, how many are you running these days?" This of course has nothing to do with a jogging ministry designed for some physical benefit. No, this question is designed exclusively for the exercise of well-tuned egos. Somewhere in our thinking exists a belief that the quantity we have contained in our worship services is in direct correlation to the impact that we are having on the Kingdom of God. Before we become too convinced of this, remember the truth telling of our European critics.

How then do numbers and impact correlate? Remember Jesus' teaching on yeast?

The Kingdom of heaven is like yeast that a woman took and mixed into a large amount of flour until it worked all through the dough. (Matthew 13:33)

Numbers and influence correlate only to the extent of our participation in God's Kingdom agenda. When we ask the question, "How many are you running?" in many cases we are simultaneously asking, "How many are you sitting?" Sitting in a sacred building and extending the Kingdom of God can be two very different activities. In fact, often they are polar opposites. If "running" involves listening to truth but not transforming our priorities, then we, too, are stuck in the deceptive make-believe world of the Third Kingdom.

Do not merely listen to the word, and so deceive yourselves. Do what it says. (James 1:22)

What if our church saw as its goal the Kingdom of God instead of the number of bodies it gathered and organized into straight rows? The "how many are we sitting?" question might more accurately be asked as, "How many are we sidelining?" How many have been benched? How many have we kept off the Kingdom playing field in order to fill our stands and stroke our collective egos? How many members of the body of Christ need to be put on the disabled list in order for us to afford newer and grander stadiums? How many have we effectively convinced that their spectator-like attendance and their tithe is all that God is ever going to hold them accountable for on the Day of Judgment? And so we keep score; nickels and noses are the tokens that count. And so that is what we count.

But has a pesky question like this one ever nagged at your spirit, "Who can build a stadium big enough to contain what God desires to do?" If it has, perhaps there is room for an alternative reality for a truly Kingdom design.

So we get to the heart of deconstructing our second myth. How can it be that in the very places where there is so much potential for the Kingdom of God to be expanded, that it seems to be, by most means of measurement, shrinking? Shouldn't church attendance be the best indicator of God's reign over his people?

Maybe not.

"How many are you giving?"

The Sanctuary was a dream, an idealist's fantasy and a labor of love. From the beginning we knew that God was leading us to be very "Kingdom-esque" in our approach to this new church we were planting just west of Toronto. We really had to be; God was setting us up.

We committed to God that every life He brought to our movement did not belong to us but to Him. Each life was His for His Kingdom, not ours.

We had no money or funding structures as this small team prepared to move from three different cities across North America, so God inspired us to commit that every dollar that came our way would be for His Kingdom, not ours. God set us up.

We didn't have a core group—we really only knew one family in the area where we were moving (who agreed to host our three families in their townhouse for an indeterminate period of time—our first hippie commune). We committed to God that every life He brought to our movement did not belong to us, but to Him. Each life was His for His Kingdom, not ours.

We looked around and saw that the largest church of any stripe across Canada had fewer than 5,000 people (which happened to be situated more than 2,000 miles west of us), and here we sat in a densely populated metropolitan area of almost six million people. Was church growth with its inherent principle of addition going to make much of a difference? What if God blessed us and we were able to grow twice as large as any church had ever grown in the history of this nation? What is that compared to the spiritual need? Spit. God once again inspired us to vow to Him that we would live out His Kingdom principle of multiplication; we would give ourselves away in establishing new, multiplying congregations. Once again, God set us up.

God inspired us to begin with this picture in our hearts: "a growing group of friends giving ourselves away to build the Kingdom of God."

We drafted a launch strategy, which included planting our first daughter congregation in year three. What God meant by "giving ourselves away" was that we would begin planting four daughter congregations simultaneously in our first year of existence. Plenty of criticism came our way for jeopardizing our base by diverting funds and energy away from this infant mother. What rang louder in our ears were Jesus' words about how you live in His Kingdom:

> *For whoever wants to save his life will lose it, but whoever loses his life for me and for the gospel will save it.* (Mark 8:35)

For too many years I had insulated myself from the full impact of Kingdom passages like this by using them as directions on how to get into the Kingdom of Heaven instead of Jesus' intended guidelines for how you function when you are a part of His Kingdom. If we were to be a small part of advancing the Kingdom of God in our corner of the planet, we would have to relearn many of Jesus' teachings. The upcoming chapters share a little of the story.

THE TEMPORARY ETERNAL

I love churches. I love seeing a group of wide-eyed Christ followers getting together and figuring out how to bring Jesus to their community, or more accurately, how to help people see Jesus who is already there. I have given my life to this cause. There is nothing more fulfilling than to see a coalition of brand new disciples of Jesus in some school gymnasium or community center, gathering and praising God—and then dispersing and serving their world.

> As much as I love the church, I have to remind myself that the church was never meant to be the goal. The body of Christ is a tool to advance the Kingdom of God, not the goal of the Kingdom of God.

Here is the rub. As much as I love the local church, I have to remind myself that the local church was never meant to be the goal. The local body of Christ is a *tool* to advance the Kingdom of God, not the *goal* of the Kingdom of God. Local churches are temporary; they have a life cycle, a shelf life. No doubt many have long exceeded that shelf life and still operate under the designation of church, but have long ceased to operate within the constraints of God's Kingdom. Churches can be reduced to man-centered organizations but the Kingdom of God cannot. Should a church find itself functioning in the miserable state of pragmatic human-centered strategic planning, it is in exceedingly dangerous territory. There is no Third Kingdom. If local churches do not advance the Kingdom of God, they reduce it. We march with Jesus or we march against Him.

The Kingdom of God is eternal. It began before time started ticking and will continue long after our planet has expired. Have you visited one of the seven churches in Revelation? Not a lot happening I understand. How about all the congregations that the apostle Paul started—have you ever attended one of those? No? Apparently their shelf life had expired as well. What about the effect of these congregations on the eternal Kingdom of God? What Christ follower of this century has not had their mind renewed and transformed simply because a group of followers of Jesus existed two millennia ago. The Kingdom of God has been forcefully advanced.

I bet brother Rufus' saintly mother had no idea of her eternal impact.†

So how should we then live?

It's church budget time, or it's make-the-hard-call time, or it's who-is-going-to-be-our-new-leader time. What is the right decision for any church to consider: to preserve our institutions or to extend the Kingdom of God? If saving our lives means losing our lives, then what do decisions of institutional preservation over God's Kingdom intentions imply?

If the local church is a temporal tool and the Kingdom of God is the eternal goal, then it follows that institutional security over Kingdom advancement is a deliberate choice for the dark side. No doubt some would object by asserting that seasons of self-absorbed entrenchment are necessary for the greater good of long term sustainability. This is an all-too-common refrain, but what does it say of our ecclesiology (view of the church)? Is the greater good the survival of the institution? As a local church do we have seasons where we walk with God building His Kingdom, but from time to time we take breaks to recover? If Jesus is the Head of the body charged with the sole task of Kingdom build-

---

†See the biblical mentioning of Rufus in Romans 16:13.

ing, isn't He capable of sustaining His body while marching on His mission? I hope so.

Maybe someday we can ask Rufus' mama.

One final thought. Have you ever noticed that we always talk about what is important to us? If something really excites us, people around us generally hear about it. Maybe the most sincere test of how big this Kingdom agenda is to Jesus is through the sheer volume of his teaching. Should our theology of the church and the Kingdom of God be influenced by the fact that in the gospels we have only three recorded mentions of the word "church" from Jesus' lips, while at the same time we hear Jesus teaching on the "Kingdom of God" or the "Kingdom of Heaven" eighty-four times? That might be worth examining.

GREAT BIG BOOKENDS

What church planter doesn't love the book of Acts? I have no idea how many times I have read through this account of the churches' origins. As a young man, my pastor (who, coincidentally, was another church planter) encouraged me to read a chapter of Acts each day with whatever other reading of God's Word I did for my personal worship. Again, I have no idea how many messages I have preached from the book of Acts. I know for certain that on two occasions I have systematically preached through the entire book. Shakespeare said that "familiarity breeds contempt," but when it comes to the drama of the expansion of the early church—no way!

On my most recent series of thirty-three messages through Acts called "Completely Irreligious, Yet Radically Christian," I got stuck on message number one. I was getting all revved up for the famous verse eight of the first chapter when seemingly out of nowhere verse three appeared and almost lifted in 3-D off the page.

My agenda for that particular Sunday was to talk about God's plan for global evangelization, power from God's Spirit and marching orders for the world. We've all heard the message, but try as I might I couldn't get to verse eight. Verse three just wouldn't get out of the way.

Think about this. Jesus had just spent a little over three years in almost constant contact with His disciples. He taught them amazing things about how the universe works. Most of the time His friends just didn't get it. Then came the horrific execution. His friends didn't see that coming either. And then the really big surprise—Jesus became *un-dead*! Get out!

And along came verse three:

After His suffering, He showed Himself to these men and gave many convincing proofs that He was alive. He appeared to them over a period of forty days and spoke about the Kingdom of God. (Acts 1:3)

Now picture this: The recently dead and now alive Jesus bends over backward to convince His friends that He was indeed physically alive and well in the state of Judea. From there He had everyone's attention. Better than that, they had *His* attention! For forty days Jesus and His friends hung out. Jesus taught. They believed. Who wouldn't believe every word that comes from this man's lips? And what did Jesus single out as the most important subject in the universe for His friends to understand? Discipleship? Evangelism? Leadership? Missions? Church planting? How to be a better apostle? No. The Kingdom of God. Lessons one through forty were all on this singular focus.

And so that is how the book of Acts starts out.

How does it end? Three guesses.

For two whole years Paul stayed there in his own rented house and welcomed all who came to see him. Boldly and without hindrance he preached the Kingdom of God and taught about the Lord Jesus Christ. (Acts 28:30-31)

The centrality of the message of the
Kingdom of God is the vehicle on which the
early church rammed through spiritual
barrier after barrier.

Bookends. Great big Kingdom bookends. The centrality of the message of the Kingdom of God is the vehicle on which the early church rammed through spiritual barrier after barrier. The Acts of the Holy Spirit (as some prefer to name this book) are acts of Kingdom expansion—darkness pushed back with great Spiritual power, light emerging where it had never been seen. Static religious systems of various persuasions tried desperately to hold their ground, but they were no matches for the Kingdom of God in power. The Kingdom of God was very good news. The church had something to say. Good News was proclaimed in both authoritative word and miraculous deed.

If the resurrected Jesus spent forty days in our churches, I wonder what He would have to say?

THE PARABLE OF THE PRETTY GURUS

Economists forever remember the conclusion of the twentieth century by the descriptor that U.S. Federal Reserve Chair Alan Greenspan coined as the age of "irrational exuberance." Technology equities knew only one direction—straight up. Telecom stocks were always big winners. This was the age of the information revolution—there will never be enough bandwidth! Scoop 'em while you can! Companies like Enron and WorldCom were the darlings of the industry. Quarter after quarter, they continued to make their shareholders wealthier. Sure there were some naysayers whispering negative sentiments like "bubble" and "crash." Sour grapes could explain most of the murmuring to be sure.

Before the age of irrational exuberance, there once lived a man of great influence. When he spoke, people stopped what they were doing and listened. His name became synonymous with skillful, shrewd, consistent investing. And he, Warren Buffet, became a very wealthy man by understanding the time-tested principles of the stock market, and never, ever straying from them. He was a very important man before the age of exuberance.

With the new age came new gurus. Much prettier ones. Hipper advisors who loved lattes and manicures and casual Fridays. Young men and women with new celebrity status appeared regularly on the ever-expanding array of business shows. They told us what to buy. We bought. How could we go wrong? They were on TV!

Way in the background, in some dark paneled office, at his desk sitting on a leather chair, facing a black telephone with a dial, sat Mr. Buffet—a relic of the old regime. He certainly wasn't pretty. He drank ordinary black coffee. Never had a manicure. You can only guess what he wore on Fridays. We could put up with all that, but what we couldn't stomach was how he talked. He had some strange idea that share prices were not all that the stock market was about. That there were certain fundamentals that determined the value of a company. *Who cares about companies*, we thought, *we're into the stock market!* He kept mumbling something about, what was the word? Value? Who knows?

Speaking as a part owner of WorldCom, I now care. My investment in that company has grown to somewhere around three cents. Not bad. It could have been worse.

The pretty latte drinking gurus are, for the most part, gone. The dinosaurs are back. Casual Fridays now include a tie and a jacket. Exuberance has lost its wind. And all is as it should be—including me and my three cents.

What can we learn from the decade of irrational exuberance? Anything?

Our Warren Buffets are antiques like
A. W. Tozer, Oswald Chambers and
Dietrich Bonhoeffer. They spoke of strange
things like "costly grace" and "intimacy
with God" and the strangest of them all,
"absolute surrender."

Certainly we can recognize ourselves in it, can't we? Our Warren Buffets are antiques like A. W. Tozer, Oswald Chambers and Dietrich Bonhoeffer. They spoke of strange things like "costly grace" and "intimacy with God" and the strangest of them all, "absolute surrender." We weren't sure what they were talking about, but we instinctively knew that it wasn't easy. Probably wasn't much fun either. So we looked for new teachers. Prettier ones.

We found them. Some put out a paperback every three months. They could tell us everything that we needed to know. Some even had conferences. Big ones. We went and bought the books and changed our churches and knew that good things were just around the corner.

But the more we changed, the less we changed.

Surely giving our worship style an extreme makeover should do the trick, so we spent money and bought things with blinking green lights that came in black cases and chased out all the old folks. Didn't need them anyway.

But the more we changed, the less we changed.

Ah, we forgot ambiance. We forgot that at the conference they told us we need ambiance. Tons of it. So we brought in Starbucks and leather lounge chairs and flat panel television monitors and chased out all the poor folks. Didn't need them anyway.

But the more we changed, the less we changed.

What could we be missing? Of course, how could we be so naïve? We need relevance! So we hauled out the pew Bibles and installed a couple jumbo screens and spoke on potty training and gardening and a thousand messages on happy marriages and we chased out all the single people. Didn't need them anyway.

Before we learned about relevance and
ambiance and methods to get married white
guys in our buildings, we used to talk
about other things. Things like prayer.
Things like mystery

How can it be that the more we change, the less we change? Maybe we're not changing the right things? Maybe the change we need can't be found while we are busy amusing ourselves to death one conference at a time. Maybe the change that is needed is us?

Let's go back to the dinosaurs. Before we learned about relevance and ambiance and methods to get married white guys in our buildings, we used to talk about other things. Things like prayer. Things like mystery (and not just so we can have candles and couches in our sacred warehouses). We talked about the Gospel. We used to talk about the poor and the sick and helpless. Some even did more than just talk. Some acted.

But that was when the dinosaurs roamed the earth. They talked about inputs; we talk about outputs. They talked about prayer; we talk about parking lots. They talked about the crucified life; we talk about critical mass. They talked about knowing God; we talk about booking Christian celebrities. They talked about the Kingdom of God. We talk about expanding our brand.

We didn't always see the difference, but I think that we see it now.

And it seems to some that the only way that we know how to turn back the tide is to organize and use our political clout as a partisan force for sacred respectability. Nothing learned, we concentrate our limited attention spans by focusing yet again on the legislating the outputs and ignoring the internal spiritual inputs which drive them.

Apparently, there is still more Kingdom ground to be lost.

Where do oak trees come from?

Before I sound too smug, let me reveal another weakness. I see the big bad wolf a mile away. I usually miss *"the little foxes."* (Song of Solomon 2:15)

Remember when I mentioned how, as we began The Sanctuary, we clearly saw God setting us up? We had no doubt that God was up to something very special.

Garry and Anita Kolb, originally from Kansas, more recently from Winnipeg, Manitoba; Jim and Joy Danielson, a typical story, California boy meets Montreal girl by way of Germany; and Laura and myself, recent owners of a "dream home" and joyful pastor of a really a wonderful church we planted in Calgary, Alberta, all set out for an exploratory meeting in the Greater Toronto Area. We each had our story.

We arrived on a long weekend in May and took different modes of transportation to the home of the one family that we knew, Barry and LaWanda Bonney. They welcomed us with open arms and we settled in for some introductions (had they known that we would soon be overstaying our welcome by three or four months, they might not have been so friendly!)

After fifteen minutes of getting to know one another, I sensed that we desperately needed to pray. We were obviously glad to be together, but the elephant in the room was that we were all scared to death. We had families that were pretty important to us—and this all seemed way too impossible. Moving to one of

North America's most expensive cities and our only economic strategy was to all quit our paying jobs. We really needed to pray.

So we gathered our chairs into a circle and began to pray. I don't remember one word that anyone uttered, but I will never forget those moments in prayer. There were not many moments, but they were powerful ones. Someone said "amen." I don't remember who it was. What I do remember is the awesome sense that we were in the face of God's presence. I have never had a moment like that before, and I have never since. The air was so thick with God's presence that it felt like you could cut it with a knife. No one looked up. No one looked around. It seemed like no one dared to look at each other. We were in God's presence. We were quiet and afraid and excited all at once. There was more.

In my spirit I sensed God's Spirit speaking very specifically. It was like He had a message to impart and He was going to do it Himself. As a good Baptist boy, this all seemed way too charismatic. There were three themes that we sensed God was saying to us:

Come to this city. I promise that I will take care of you and your children.

I am going to do something that will astound you.

Do not steal my glory.

Where do you go from a moment like that? Anita Kolb, the Kansas-Winnipeg worship pastor's wife, went to the Word. Apparently she spent a sleepless night thumbing through her well-worn Bible looking for comfort and instruction.

In the morning while we were enjoying our coffee, Anita came bounding down the stairs, eyes sparkling with delight. She had something to say. She flopped open her Bible on the kitchen table to a little right of center and put her finger on a very underlined verse.

They will be called oaks of righteousness, a planting of the Lord *for the display of his splendor.* (Isaiah 61:3b)

Here we sat, coffee in hand, in the family room of the Bonney's home situated squarely in the city of Oakville. "'Oaks of righteousness.' Oakville. I get it. That's neat." But there was more to it than that. Much more. This one verse grabbed ahold of us and wouldn't soon let go. Through His quiet voice God spoke instructions to our hearts and we knew from that day on what our Kingdom assignment was to be about:

His Dream: "Oaks of Righteousness." Transformed lives and new congregations with Kingdom DNA.

His Methodology: It was to be "a planting of the Lord." Established through the sole authority of our King.

His Condition: We were to have one focus—to "display His splendor."

And so we believed Him. We went back to our homes, resigned our positions, sold our houses, and moved to the land of God's promise, homeless and unemployed, and commissioned by the King.

And then we went to town. A congregation of un-churched "Kingdom Seekers" appeared seemingly out of thin air. With amazement we would watch a stream of minivans and sedans pour into the parking lot of the high school we occupied. A cafeteria turned house of worship, complete with hard Formica benches, was filled with the curious and the spiritually hungry. Lives became connected with their Maker. It was as the King had promised, and it was unbelievable.

We talked multiplication from Sunday one, and people began to get it. Phone calls came regularly from far away places and from next door. God was leading family after family to make huge faith steps and incredible sacrifices in order to join this merry band, and we began to multiply.

On a large wall in our home we had pinned up a map of the Greater Toronto Area with push pins marking our outposts as we began to dream of Kingdom conquest. We imagined ourselves as those early apostles—full of grit and gumption, boldly marching toward Rome.

I was sure the King was pleased.

Well, not totally. I wanted to be. I tried hard to be sure and certain. But I had women problems. Not the usual sort that sidelines so many men of the cloth. Women problems of an entirely different kind. There were a band of sisters, one not knowing the other, who, at the most inappropriate time (for from my perspective, there are precious few appropriate times for such a discussion) would say, "What about the first three verses of Isaiah 61?" "Girls," I thought to myself, "What do girls know about the manly art of outpost construction."

So I continued my exploits trying hard to keep the substance of our vision firmly removed from its context. Yet try as I might, I couldn't shake off the words that these women believed. They were hard to shake off. Why? They were the very words that our King used to inaugurate his own Kingdom agenda:

The Spirit of the Sovereign Lord *is on me,*
because the Lord *has anointed me*
to preach Good News to the poor.
He has sent me to bind up the brokenhearted,
to proclaim freedom for the captives
and release from darkness for the prisoners,
to proclaim the year of the Lord's *favor*
and the day of vengeance of our God,
to comfort all who mourn,
and provide for those who grieve in Zion—
to bestow on them a crown of beauty

instead of ashes,
the oil of gladness
instead of mourning,
and a garment of praise
instead of a spirit of despair. (Isaiah 61:1-3a)

Whenever we focus on the goals over the
integrity of the process, we will always be
tempted to produce the fruit ourselves.
God expands His Kingdom.

Those pesky little foxes (I speak of Songs 2:15, not of my female advisors.) I had my eye on the big bad wolf and I tripped over the sneaky fox. I thought that we could advance the Kingdom of God by avoiding the self-centered ambitions of the modern church. Instead I found myself repeating a slightly more spiritually sophisticated version of the same aberration—focusing on outputs and neglecting the inputs. This was a mistake our King was unwilling to make. The Kingdom of God can never be expanded apart from the context from which God's Kingdom agenda springs. "Oaks of righteousness" are the byproduct of the Kingdom activity of extending God's grace. Whenever we focus on the goals over the integrity of the process, we will always be tempted to produce the fruit ourselves. God expands His Kingdom. His subjects do what they see their King doing.

What does "Christian" mean? We know that it means "Little Christ." We know that it was originally dished-out as an insult. "Look at those people; they're acting just like that radical Jesus guy who got what he had coming. Little Christs. Walking around like a bunch of do-gooders. When will they ever learn?"

No one really expected much to come from this Little Christ sect anyway. They did everything wrong. If they were going to create another religion—at least do it right! The first rule of religion building is consolidation. Gather your resources in a central system of control. Protect them and add to them when you can. These Little Christs did exactly the opposite. They gave away stuff. Some gave away everything (how sustainable is a model like that!). The law of religion building understands the principle of giving, but you have got to get something for it. "We'll give you the secret security code to the locked gates of heaven. You give us your attendance and a prescribed amount of cash." That's how decent religions are built. You take what you get, courageously protect it, and you stack it as high as you can. Consolidate. And *voilà*, you've got yourself a sustainable world-class religion.

So really, the Little Christ movement was of no great threat. They lacked a base (everyone knows that you need a base) and they seemed to stubbornly resist the notion of consolidation. It all seemed so strangely pagan to them. I suppose that is the kind of religion you get when you leave it to uneducated fishermen.

But the Little Christ movement continued to give itself away. Expecting nothing in return, they brought Good News to the poor. They found those who had broken hearts, and with care and love they mended each heart. They found people who were addicted, and they showed them the way of freedom. They found those who had no hope, who were mourning, and they gave them comfort by showing them the hope that they had discovered. They found people who the world considered worthless, and by the sheer force of this love that emanated from within them, these "worthless" people became strangely desirable. They found people in every class of society who were despairing because of an emptiness inside, and, from the example of their selfless lives, those despairing people were transforming into praising people, and in turn became Little Christs themselves.

Breaking all the tried and tested rules of religion building, the Little Christs followed the lead of their King. One act of selfless sacrifice inspired another. One transformed life led to another. In 300 years the most remarkable thing had happened—a peaceful revolution had taken place.

The Kingdom of Darkness tried to stop it with marginalization, but it seemed like the Little Christs could care less. Statements like "we have to obey God, rather than men" seemed to roll off their lips like a well-rehearsed creed. They didn't seem to care that their neighbors thought of them as a bit odd. It seemed that in time as their neighbors joined their number, they behaved equally as odd.

But darkness had something else up its perverse sleeve. We'll turn up the heat. Certainly persecution will end their influence. But with every Little Christ they put down with a sword, ten more would rise up in his place. The more ruthless the means, the more resolute the movement became. The revolutionaries seemed unstoppable. As the Christians continued to give themselves away to one another and to the communities they inhabited, the Kingdom of God expanded.

For over 300 years, the dominion of darkness steadily lost territory. Marginalization and persecution seemed only to increase the influence of these Little Christs. Hell was very afraid. "How can we get to the very heart of this movement and kill it?", the enemy schemed.

We can see their answer in the history books. Hell's solution to the problem of the Christian revolution was consolidation. In 313 A.D., we became a world-class religion. The movement was over in one edict of preservation. Some might have thought that this was the year that the Little Christs won. We were now legitimate. We now had control and power. But in truth, this is the year that the movement began to surrender Kingdom territory en masse. Consolidation always does.

On the outside, things never looked better. We now had buildings and professional clergy and legitimacy and freedom. It was now easy to be a Little Christ. No sacrifice required. No more insults either. The world loved us—we were popular. Our numbers swelled. Everybody wanted to be a Little Christ. Well actually, nobody called us Little Christs anymore; that was a bit provincial. We were no longer a rag-tag movement of revolutionaries—we were the ones with power!

Well again that wasn't quite true. Certainly we now had political power, but what had happened to that other power we used to have? That power that changed things from the inside. Now, it seemed that we could only change the exteriors of things.

How sad it was that the Little Christs forgot what their leader had taught them about receiving illegitimate power. The Kingdom of Darkness tried to sideline Jesus with power in His own season of temptation. Jesus smelled the whiff of sulfur a mile off. He didn't bite (Matthew 4:8-11).

The Little Christs forgot about what their leader taught them about popularity. Being popular in the culture may mean that the dominion of Darkness doesn't find us all that threatening. Darkness doesn't need to waste sweat on the new brand of Christianity—it's not really its enemy.

Jesus taught the real Little Christs about what cultural popularity really means:

If you belonged to the world, it would love you as its own. As it is, you do not belong to the world, but I have chosen you out of the world. That is why the world hates you. Remember the words I spoke to you: 'No servant is greater than his master.' If they persecuted me, they will persecute you also. (John 15:19-20)

Our efforts of consolidation have reduced
us from a counterculture movement of Little
Christs to a religion preoccupied with how
many we sit in our bleachers.

Our efforts of consolidation have reduced us from a counterculture movement of Little Christs to a religion preoccupied with how many we sit in our cozy bleachers. We build auditoriums with comfy seats and theater-quality multimedia and try our best to disciple our constituency. Except, disciples are to follow, and we are not going anywhere. We are consolidating. We are no threat. We don't do anything threatening. We can't.

And therein lies the great oxymoronic paradox.

In our fascination with church growth, we have unintentionally stripped away the spiritual power for the Kingdom to grow. It's become one of those sneaky little foxes destroying the vine.

It hasn't always been like this. And it's certainly not like this everywhere. But for many of us, believing the myth of church growth is our greatest temptation.

As our European friends taught us, Christian brand-expansion apart from community transformation means the Kingdom of God has functionally decreased.

We have lost enough ground.

CHAPTER 3

THE MYTH OF KINGDOM TURF
The Assumption of Alien Allies

It is possible to unknowingly value the Kingdom of God before understanding the value of its Source: the King.

There are two basic schools of thought on how to effectively start a new community of faith that will have an evangelistic impact on its community. The go-to move for most church planters is what I call the *"gather and go"* method. You gather some dedicated, trained, faithful, tithing leaders who know what church is all about, and send them out to reach the community. Intuitively, it seems the way to go, especially if one has a limited funding runway. If the greatest good is financial self-sustainability, we are to deploy this methodology before the bathtub of resources is depleted. The church must be up and self-sustaining before we hear the last gurgle of promised resources sucking down the drain. By concentrating strategies on gathering the already evangelized, most of our financial and leadership needs are solved from day one. Now we are free to point the waiting army toward the great commission.

The difficult task of the "gather and go" method is the *going* part. It is complex from two different directions. First, many seasoned veterans of the faith are already convinced that evangelism is difficult, if not nearly impossible, and we should not expect many to respond. We often approach this assignment pre-loaded with a culture of defeat. The primary reason for this "impossibility" is that most have long since distanced themselves from real friendships with the lost. Second, from the target community's perspective, they instinctively know that they do not fit in. They intuitively understand that they are different; they do not know what the core team knows. Someone makes a biblical allusion and before he is finished, most of the room is already nodding in agreement—the newbie has no context to piece things together. They feel like first-graders surrounded by a roomful of twelfth-graders. As a result of this "differentness," they tend to bounce off and not stick in any high ratios.

There is another way. It actually illustrates the assumption of this chapter. It is what I call the *"go and gather"* method. Instead of gathering a group of seasoned Christian leaders, developing your value statements, your vision statements, and your mission statements that will be used to define your culture, why not include the community you are trying to reach in the process? I can almost hear the objections of some already: "Ask the unregenerate to advise the regenerate? That is like asking thieves to give advice to security detail at Fort Knox—it's just not reliable intelligence." The myth of Kingdom turf is alive and well in many hearts.

Let me illustrate the "go and gather" method from my own experience.

Before we started The Sanctuary in 2001 we had a core team of four committed families. From previous experiences in church planting, we had made the commitment to "close the door" to further evangelicals, and concentrate on building a launch team that reflected our audience—the lost of Oakville. We began to initiate relationships with people through natural channels of business and neighborhood. We engaged in some ministry projects that put us face-to-face in relationship with other men and women who were curious about this "thing" that we were starting. We spent six months cultivating relationships with people in order to develop the beginnings of trust.

Six months in we had a pretty good list of names of friendships we had developed at varying levels, people we believed trusted us, or at the very least, trusted our good intentions. We made our first withdrawal from that trust account: we asked if they would gather in a community center, on a weekday evening, and give us some advice. We explained that two things would take place. First, we would have a meal together, and second, I was going to ask one simple question. No one would be embarrassed or put on the spot. We valued and needed their thoughts.

We thought that if everyone came that we had spoken to, we could have around sixty adults that evening.

The evening came. Together we prepared a meal of lasagna, salad, bread, tea and coffee. We had arranged eight round tables that sat eight around the room and prepared place settings. The investments of friendship and trust became evident as we watched single moms, divorced men, married couples, neighbors, our insurance broker, our realtor, our lawyer, people we had first met in ministry projects—all walk into the room. In that room sat sixty friends eating lasagna.

These people were connected to one of our four core families and not necessarily to one another, so the conversation at the tables was stilted at the beginning. That was about to change. It was now time for the second part of the evening.

The question.

I stood and interrupted the various conversations happening, thanked them for coming, and thanked them in advance for their valuable input. I explained that I was about to ask a question, and would like each table to discuss the question and elect a spokesman to share their response. Everything was clear. Here was the question:

How would you describe your ideal spiritual community?

Elaborate by explaining what is important? What is not? What is significant? What is irrelevant? What does it do? What doesn't it do? Paint a picture.

It was pretty quiet in that room for the first seconds. This was a question that most normal people rarely discuss aloud. There were some awkward seconds. Soon one brave soul at a table would venture out, and then another. In almost no time at all the room was buzzing with animated conversation.

About fifteen minutes into this exercise I once again stood up and interrupted. It was time to report. I was nervous and excited all at once. I expected to gain some intelligence that would help us shape our future, but I was not expecting to hear what I was about to hear.

God had created a longing in their hearts for
an authentic worshipping community and had
given them the words and pictures
to describe it.

Unchurched person after unchurched person stood up and shared a picture of the ideal spiritual community. These were the three most common themes:

1. God would be important every day, not on just one day.
2. It would be a spiritual community that cared for the physical, emotional, and spiritual needs of one another.
3. It would be a spiritual community that took responsibility for the greater community.

I stood there flabbergasted as I heard these people with little to no Christian experience articulate a healthier theology of Christian community than I have found on some of our seminary campuses. God had created a longing in their hearts for an authentic worshipping community and had given them the words and pictures to describe it.

Only as the Holy Spirit could have arranged it, I had already had my index finger jammed in my Bible to hold the place open to Acts 2:42-47. I read it to these friends slowly:

> *They devoted themselves to the apostles' teaching and to the fellow-ship, to the breaking of bread and to prayer. Everyone was filled with awe, and many wonders and miraculous signs were done by the apostles. All the believers were together and had everything in common. Selling their possessions and goods, they gave to anyone as he had need. Every day they continued to meet together in the temple courts. They broke bread in their homes and ate together with glad and sincere hearts, praising God and enjoying the favor of all the people. And the Lord added to their number daily those who were being saved.* (NIV)

Now it was their turn to be amazed. These Kingdom-seekers who were able to articulate the longings of their hearts were dumbfounded to discover that the Word of God had already described spiritual community in that same way.

God had already done the work. I invited these friends to join us in building this kind of spiritual community. Since it originated from the deep places of their spirit, it was not a difficult sell. The Holy Spirit had already been at work.

Over the next twelve months we baptized 52 of our new friends.

Over the next nine years, these friends would "give themselves away" nine more times, multiplying themselves into ten congregations in the Toronto area.

Over the next nine years, these friends would give time and resources and leadership away to start two church planting organizations, which together have started numerous churches within our city.

To God be the glory.

THE MYTH OF KINGDOM TURF

The history of religion seems in many ways to be a history of competing ideologies, each asserting the audacious claim of having God on their side.

In 1987, Laura and I married. A few months later, we moved to the town where I would be attending seminary. We heard about a new church plant that was beginning and sensed that God wanted us to be a part of it during our seminary years. Laura was a teacher. To a new church plant, that's like raw meat to a dog. Two Sundays in, Laura was at the front of the auditorium, surrounded by little children, delivering little pearls of biblical wisdom to her nose-picking and carpet-squirming audience. The children listened too.

Laura is a St. Louis girl through and through. That happened also to be the year the St. Louis Cardinals faced the Minnesota Twins in the World Series. St. Louis was losing and Laura was distressed. It really showed one Sunday.

Laura was delivering a "sermonette" (that's what our Baptist women do) on the theme of persistence. The illustration was close at hand. Laura said, "The St. Louis Cardinals are losing the World Series. Do you think that they should quit?" The dutiful ensemble echoed in unison "No!"

Good answer, Laura thought. The warm-up complete, Laura delivered the pitch.

"Whenever we feel tired or sad or discouraged, we shouldn't quit either. What should we do instead?" Timmy, the skinny one doing somersaults during the presentation, immediately stood to his full three feet six inches, shot up his arm and exclaimed "I know! I know!" Laura said, "Yes, Timmy?" And then came the one thing that instills pride in every teacher—the perfect answer. Timmy looked at Laura with bright eyes beaming and said confidently "Pray."

Timmy, in his short experience at life, had mastered the cure for sadness and discouragement. Laura, being fully confident that all had gathered the full significance of Timmy's answer, went ahead and tied up the loose ends to make a dramatic conclusion to the lesson on persistence.

And then came the time for prayer. Laura asked, "Who would like to pray and ask God to help us not to quit when we get tired or sad or discouraged?" Again, Timmy, not to be ignored, began to jump up and down exclaiming, "Me, me, me, me!" Laura, as if she had any other choice, said, "All right, Timmy. Please pray."

Timmy closed his eyes and clasped together his hands and with great sincerity said to God, "Dear God, please help the Cardinals to beat that other team. Amen."

Laura's point was made.

Whose side are you on?

History records that the 1987 World Series went to the Minnesota Twins. Despite the fervent and sincere prayer of Timmy, the Cardinals lost 11-5 in game seven.

As silly as it sounds, when it comes to our religion, there is a whole lot of Timmy in many of us. "Dear God, help us win this city. Amen." Or perhaps, "Dear God, the Muslims (or Methodists, or Pentecostals, or Baptists, or Catholics, or whomever the enemy) are a growing threat in our community. Help us to have the victory. Amen."

Let's face it, we all want God on our side. Who wouldn't? Do you remember Steven Spielberg's movie *The Raiders of the Lost Ark?* Nazi Germany knew that if they possessed the Ark of the Covenant, they would have God on their side and would win the war. The rules are simple. Those who have God on their team win.

God has always been pretty popular.

God, as a rule, doesn't choose sides. Instead,
God reveals Himself and then allows those
who care to choose Him.

The problem of Timmy's prayer is that God, as a rule, doesn't choose sides. Instead, God reveals Himself and then allows those who care to choose Him. That is more or less the theme of the book of Galatians. In Spielberg's movie, the Nazis thought that they could possess God. What happened? In possessing Him, they dared to look at Him and that was their end. God could not be owned.

If no one can even gaze in God's direction and survive, how can any group (even the ones with all the right theology) claim to have exclusive licensing rights to either Him or His turf? Who owns the Kingdom of God? Who, at the very least, has the most honest claim on it?

And with this, we begin to deconstruct our third Christian fable, the myth of Kingdom turf.

THE SEEKER'S SEEKER

At the heart of the preceding question, "Who has claim on Kingdom turf?" lays a theological error that the modern church has incorporated into its psyche without thought of its legitimacy or its destructive implications. Many of us, if we were honest, would say that we have a deep-seated conviction that God is on our side (the side of truth), and through us (the side of truth) He will bring about His Kingdom objectives. We are "the people of the Book." We are the remnant, the faithful, the ones who have not bowed the knee to the fluffy goddess of skepticism and all of her iniquitous descendants. We have claim.

If the standard for claim on Kingdom turf were that of theological correctness, well then, we are set. We have the advantage of some of history's best scholars who have faithfully devoted their lives to helping us to properly understand God's Word within its original context. But what if theological correctness included more than careful and sophisticated interpretation? What if it also concerned itself with the larger context of God's redemptive purpose (which is clearly observed in any honest reading of God's Word)? What if our theological correctness wasn't considered "true" until it first included the acknowledgment that God is without need of me, my church, my denomination, my subculture, or even my efforts to build His Kingdom?

What if we drew the lens back all the way until we came face to face with the obvious truth that the Sovereign God, the King of His Kingdom, is not dependent on or limited in any way by me or my tribe? He alone holds claim to the turf of His Kingdom. He is not looking for sides to join. He is seeking a people who will lay aside every other allegiance (including religious ones) and unite with Him.

For the eyes of the LORD *range throughout the earth to strengthen those whose hearts are fully committed to him.* (2 Chronicles 16:9)

The seeker's Seeker is without need of aid or assistance. In fact, the relationship between Seeker and he who is sought is counterintuitive to the minds of those who claim Kingdom turf. His redemptive purpose has at its very heart the welfare of those He seeks. The King is not recruiting warriors to help Him tip the balance in His *jihad* against darkness, but rather is seeking men and women who will find their completion in His presence. In this process, darkness is expelled by the Light of His presence and the Kingdom of God is forcefully advanced.

Even though the myth of Kingdom turf assumes as a reality the very impossibility of ownership of that which cannot be owned—it is not a new or novel delusion. It actually has had a long and storied tradition. Inherent, it would seem, is the innate compulsion to believe in the deepest part of our hearts that God is on our side. We ask for God's blessings on our plans and then we proceed without Him. We open our church's business meetings in prayer and then with all the rights of democracy begin to establish our will over someone else's and say that in this process, God has spoken. For some reason, we think we should be able to declare to all that God is indeed on our side.

This dark compulsion to reduce God's stature to a more convenient pocket-sized version has been the long habit of religions throughout history. Everybody wants a scaled-down "God-esque" action figure that can be produced on a moment's notice to demonstrate piety and correctness.

If only God would cooperate.

THE IRRELIGIOUS RABBI

The word on Jesus was out. The carpenter's son had a growing reputation as an astounding speaker and even a miracle worker. Now he was coming home. With full rabbi status, Jesus walks into his familiar hometown synagogue and is given the honor of leadership over the second part of the service. The *Haptarah*, the reading of the Prophets, was the component of the service that included a message to be delivered by the rabbi. Joseph's son carefully selected one of the Isaiah scrolls, unrolled it to the section we now call chapter 61 verses one and two, stood and read:

> *The Spirit of the Lord is on me, because he has anointed me to preach Good News to the poor. He has sent me to proclaim freedom for the prisoners and recovery of sight for the blind, to release the oppressed, to proclaim the year of the Lord's favor.* (Luke 4:18-19)

Having finished reading, Jesus, with great care, re-rolled the synagogue's precious scroll, handed it back the attendant, and as was the custom, sat down to preach. All eyes were upon him. Expectations were exceedingly high, for the word on Jesus was out.

What happened next was not expected. Instead of doing what rabbis do—explain the meaning of what was read—the carpenter's son did something that no one had ever seen. He didn't explain anything. Instead, he made this astonishing claim,

Today this scripture is fulfilled in your hearing. (Luke 4:21)

Jesus never worked a miracle on demand.
Convenient pocket-sized gods might do that
sort of thing, but Jesus wasn't one of them

As happens often in religious assemblies, *what* was being said is of less significance to *how* it was being said. The *how* it was being said part amazed the congregation. "He's amazing. These gracious words seem to just flow off his lips. His reputation is well earned; who has ever heard anyone like him before? Such authority. Such command. We could sit and listen to this rabbi all day long! Who would have ever thought that little Jesus would grow up to be . . ."

And then the penny dropped.

Isn't this Joseph's son? (Luke 4:22)

The *what* was being said part was finally kicking in and Jesus knew what they were thinking. "If you are who you say you are, work a miracle to prove it—homeboy." But Jesus never worked a miracle on demand. Convenient pocket-sized gods might do that sort of thing, but Jesus wasn't one of them. Instead, He countered,

I tell you the truth no prophet is accepted in his hometown. (Luke 4:24)

Jesus declared a universal axiom and then stated that He would not be an exception to it. One generation ridicules a man; the next generation builds a monument to him. This is especially true for those who grow up amongst us. "He can't be that great because we know him" is the self-demeaning sentiment at the heart of their skepticism. They would tempt Jesus for more. As in the wilderness, so here, Jesus so completely limited Himself in His humanity that He would live in subjection to all of man's confines. There would be no miracles for the unbelieving religious. To drive His point home, Jesus makes two remarkable statements that speak to the myth of turf:

> *I assure you that there were many widows in Israel in Elijah's time, when the sky was shut for three and a half years and there was a severe famine throughout the land. Yet Elijah was not sent to any of them, but to a widow in Zarephath in the region of Sidon. And there were many in Israel with leprosy in the time of Elisha the prophet, yet not one of them was cleansed—only Naaman the Syrian.* (Luke 4:25-27)

Jesus didn't pull any punches. Even though, at Elijah's word, it did not rain for three and one half years, during that parching drought, Elijah wasn't sent to a widow from Israel, but to a foreigner—an outsider. Israel had rejected Elijah, but through her faith, the woman of Sidon received a great blessing from God (see 1 Kings 12:9ff).

The congregation at the synagogue wasn't impressed. "Why would Jesus say this? Is he against us? Is he against Israel?"

To make sure that His point was not lost on anyone, Jesus cited another example. Despite the many lepers in Israel, only one was healed by Elisha—Naaman, the outsider. Again, the controlling factor was faith, not pedigree. The lepers of Israel ignored Elisha, but acting in faith to the revelation he had received, Naaman alone received cleansing from God (see 2 Kings 5:1ff).

Jesus' point could not be missed. No one was impressed with *how* he spoke any longer. The *how* and the *what* had all come together in one amazing scorcher of a carpenter-turned-rabbi sermon like no one had ever heard. Outsiders would be blessed if they responded to the revelation that God gives. Insiders would be ignored, passed-over, disregarded (or worse) if they did not demonstrate faith in God's revelation. Others, any others, even Gentiles, would receive a blessing from Him, but His hometown, through their own unbelief, would be completely passed over.

To infer that outsiders could be objects of God's favor, even more than the carpenter's own people, was an unforgivable statement. It was something that could not be tolerated. This irreligious rabbi must be stopped with any and every possible means.

All the people in the synagogue were furious when they heard this. They got up, drove him out of the town, and took him to the brow of the hill on which the town was built, in order to throw him down the cliff. But he walked right through the crowd and went on his way. (Luke 4:28-30)

The only miracle Jesus' hometown would see was His miraculous exit.

From our vantage point looking backward into history, we comprehend the Jew-Gentile message of Jesus with little trouble. We understand this first century application that salvation is available by faith to all, independent of national origins. What we find thornier is to take Jesus' principle and translate it into the issues of the twenty-first century. We no longer struggle with the distinctions of Jew or Gentile, Norwegian or North Korean, American or African; the atoning sacrifice of Jesus is for all peoples.

But we have other blind spots.

Jesus, using the examples of the widow of Zarephath and the leper Naaman of Syria, intended far more emotional punch to the hometown crowd than merely a controversy of ethnicity. Jesus spoke of the distinctions of faith and unbelief and of obedience and insubordination. As in Jesus' examples, these distinctions have little to do with the simple divisions of race and religion and have more to do with the actions defined by light and darkness. The widow and the leper existing outside of the established religious forms, found themselves cooperating with God and thereby advancing His Kingdom while those within the form of religion chose a path of disobedience.

To consider ourselves as claimants to
God's Kingdom because of our theological
statements proves that we are close cousins
to Jesus' hometown neighbors and that
we totally missed His point.

The Gospel that we have received comes through an irreligious rabbi. To consider ourselves as claimants to God's Kingdom because of our theological statements proves that we are close cousins to Jesus' hometown neighbors and that we totally missed His point. Jesus always commends faith, never heritage or association. Confusing the two invariably produces a deviant form of Christianity with its predictable religious offspring: "sacrifice without mercy."

SECTION II

Reconstructing Kingdoms

DISTINGUISHING BETWEEN FORMS AND SOURCES

We love forms. We love categories and pigeonholes and compartments. We love ways of distinguishing and classifying. It makes everything so much simpler. *This is a good thing. This is a bad thing.* All the hard work is now done. We take all the good things and put them in one pile, and name the pile "sacred". That is a very special pile indeed. We take all the bad things and put them in the stinky pile, and name it "secular." We stay well away from that pile.

The trouble with our piles is that we sometimes get things mixed up. Sometimes the things in our "sacred" pile begin to smell a bit ripe. And sometimes we can catch a very fresh whiff emanating from that pile we were told to stay away from.

The trouble with our piles is that we sometimes get things mixed up. Sometimes the things in our "sacred" pile begin to smell a bit ripe. And sometimes we can catch a very fresh whiff emanating from that pile we were told to stay away from.

Sometimes our piles and pigeonholes can be confusing.

Jesus walked into the most categorized, compartmentalized, pigeonholed culture in human history and began to actively challenge the sacred forms. Was Jesus just looking for trouble when He worked on the Sabbath, or when He neglected a ceremonial washing, or when He hung out with those who were considered unclean?

Or was Jesus teaching us something?

CHAPTER 4
KINGDOMS RECONSTITUTED

Thus far we have spent a considerable amount of time with the sole intent of deconstructing three hazardous, yet widely accepted myths of the modern evangelical church. These were:

First, we looked at *the myth of the third Kingdom:* the assumption of sides. We concluded that at any given moment I am either building the Kingdom of God or the Kingdom of Darkness.

Second, we studied *the myth of the church growth:* the assumption of lost ground. Here we observed that it is possible to participate in church expansion and unintentionally be an agent for shrinking the Kingdom of God.

Third, we observed *the myth of Kingdom turf:* the assumption of alien allies. Looking through Scripture and experience we noted that it is possible to unknowingly participate in the Kingdom of God before acknowledging the value of its Source: the King.

This effort, although helpful, is not complete. It's like knocking over a condemned building and leaving a gaping hole in the neighborhood. We haven't significantly helped the neighborhood unless some construction soon follows.

And so we construct.

FORMS MAY OCCASIONALLY MATTER

Is it possible to distinguish perfectly between
sacred and secular, choose the sacred, and
still be living in darkness?

Is it possible to distinguish perfectly between sacred and secular, choose the sacred, and still be living in darkness? Let me tell you a story.

Allan was kind of a shy kid. He never wanted to be in the foreground; he felt much more comfortable in the peanut gallery. He had a sense of humor that constantly got him in trouble in school with the little 'one liners' that he would offer at the most inappropriate time. Allan, the shy kid, spent more than his fair share of time in the principal's office.

He grew up in a family whose parents became Christ followers as adults and who lived lives that were radically transformed. They brought Allan and his sister Cathy to church every Sunday and modeled Jesus throughout the rest of the week. Soon Allan and his sister Cathy became Christ followers, too.

Allan's parents and his new church had a powerful impact on his life. God began to speak to his spirit, and soon Allan began to sense a call from God to become a pastor. This was exciting and troubling to Allan all at one time. It was exciting because God had given him a picture of what his life was going to be about. He knew in his heart of hearts that God had created him to help people understand the consequences of eternity.

But this call was troubling, too. It didn't appear to Allan that he had any of the spiritual gifts necessary to be a pastor. Worse than that, he was deathly afraid to speak in public. He was pretty sure that this was something that pastors had to do. Most of the times that he had to give a speech in high school, he would feign some kind of illness and miss that class period. When he did give an oral presentation of some kind, he would feel nauseated, as he would stammer his way through his report. Allan's speeches were usually the worst in his class. And God wanted Allan to be a pastor?

Allan had to talk with his pastor. He explained what he sensed that God was saying to him and his own confusion because of his perceived lack of gifts. Allan's pastor shared the story of his own call to ministry. Apparently he had suffered from the same affliction as a young man, and still continued to find it difficult to preach. Allan was surprised to find out that his pastor had a fear of public speaking, too. In seeing how God had used his pastor, it gave courage to Allan's sense of call.

Soon Allan graduated from high school and began to make plans for university. Sensing a call to be a pastor, Allan applied and was accepted at a Christian university. His course of studies was to be in the theological school, as he would prepare for ministry. "Introduction to Public Speaking" was on Allan's schedule for his first semester. Surely things would be different now that he was at a Christian university. But Allan's fear followed him even to a

Christian institution. Nausea in full force, he once again struggled through speech after speech, consistently receiving the lowest scores in his class. Allan thought, "God must have this wrong."

Allan got involved in a group that was responsible for booking and promoting contemporary Christian artists to play on campus. This gave him a buzz. He began to meet and get to know some of the people whose music he had spent hours listening to. As a couple of years passed, and he began to build relationships with some of these artists, he realized that some doors were opening in front of him. The Christian music industry was starting to become big, he now had many contacts, and he had proven his competence. Allan began to think, "I can serve God on a much larger platform through the doors that are open in front of me. And besides, it fits my gifts much better." Allan began to dream some big dreams.

Time passed and life just got better because Allan found the perfect girl. She was pretty and smart in one little package. Laura was an elementary education major who had a deep passion for God. One day, Laura received a class assignment to make a tombstone rubbing of a historical grave marker in the area. The two, not missing any opportunity for romance, considered this "date potential" and headed together to the oldest graveyard they could locate.

Hand in hand, the happy couple walked through the old graveyard, glancing at headstones to locate anything of historical significance. It was a beautiful, sunny spring day. Allan sat by an old walnut tree enjoying the outdoors, while Laura, paper and soft pencil in hand, continued her mission.

While Allan leaned against the tree, he noticed a grave marker lying flat in the ground, overgrown with weeds and covered with soil. He was curious. He reached over and brushed the grave marker so it was clean enough to read. What was engraved on this stone was about to change Allan's life:

"Samuel Jacobson, died 1813"

Allan thought, "Wow, that guy has been dead a long time. He lived most of his life in the 1700's." And then he had a series of thoughts (that later, he realized, didn't come from himself). "I wonder what he did for a living? A farmer, maybe? He probably had a family and worked hard and did his best." His thoughts then went down a different avenue. "I wonder who remembers old Samuel Jacobson? His children? No. They are long dead. His grandchildren? No. They've been gone a long time, too. His great-grandchildren? His great-great grandchildren?" And then Allan began to count the generations from Samuel Jacobson that had come and gone since he had walked in this community. The cold, hard, logical conclusion wasn't lost on Allan. "No one on earth knows that Samuel Jacobson ever walked on this planet."

And from that mental synapse came another—one that rang with absolute clarity in his mind. "Whatever Samuel did for himself has been forever lost. Whatever Samuel did in the Kingdom of God still remains."

Now God had Allan's full attention. He had been running from his divine assignment because he felt inadequate for the task. He rationalized his disobedience to God by justifying that the assignment that he felt more comfortable with could be technically construed as obedience from an outside onlooker.

What we learn from Allan's life is that God isn't as nearly concerned with "forms" as He is with "sources." Under the form of "sacred," Allan was preparing to live a life of disobedience to God, which can only mean that the dominion of darkness is advanced. In Allan's case, the form of sacred was largely an inconsequential designation because it belied the reality of the darkness from where it originated. Allan's pursuit was comfort, acclaim and security over the humility of walking in the King's shadow.

How do I know Allan's motivations so clearly? I know him pretty well. Allan is actually his middle name—one that I share. His first and last names are mine as well.

FORM CRITICISM

Examples abound in our culture of the
'sacred' smelling a bit funky, and the 'secular'
looking a lot like Jesus.

So, who is advancing the Kingdom of God? Someone like me who chooses to fly under the banner of sacred, yet chooses a self-indulgent path over obedience? Or someone who may wince at the designation of sacred but in obedience to the Light he is given, help the helpless? Examples abound in our culture of the sacred smelling a bit funky, and the secular looking a lot like Jesus.

Teaching on this theme was not uncommon for Jesus. The religious people were altogether enthusiastic about their forms. They had established the two-party system—theirs and ours. Our party, which had God on its side, and their party, which, by definition, had to be godless. The rules were clear. The secular was always bad and sacred was always good.

Jesus seemed to understand the rules. The problem was, He just seemed to disagree with them.

Put yourself in the picture when Jesus told the story recorded in Matthew 21:28-32. There Jesus was, having just had His authority questioned by the most significant sacred leaders of His day, offering a parable with a biting point to those who hold the sacred/secular distinction so tightly.

Jesus lobs a softball:

"What do you think? There was a man who had two sons. He went to the first and said, 'Son, go and work today in the vineyard.' "I will not,' he answered, but later he changed his mind and went. "Then the father went to the other son and said the same thing. He answered, 'I will, sir,' but he did not go."

Two sons. One son said, "Can't help you, Dad, I'm pretty busy!" But he repented and obeyed his father. The other son said, "Of course I'll obey!" But he was a no-show. Pretty simple little story. Jesus, being confident that all had grasped his story, asked the sacred leaders a question of comprehension:

"Which of the two did what his father wanted?"

Easy story. Easy question. "Must be some kind of a trick", some might have thought, "Jesus never asks easy questions." Taking advantage of Jesus letting them off easy, the sacred leaders replied as a chorus:

"The first," they answered.

It must have felt good to get the right answer. The sacred leaders carefully analyzed the story and gave the only logical solution. It was easy, but it still felt good.

The good feeling lasted about 1.5 seconds—the time it took for Jesus to inhale before He let out this sharp little observation:

Jesus said to them, "I tell you the truth, the tax collectors and the prostitutes are entering the kingdom of God ahead of you. For John came to you to show you the way of righteousness, and you did not believe him, but the tax collectors and the prostitutes did. And even after you saw this, you did not repent and believe him." (Matthew 21:28-32)

Was Jesus really saying this? The secular world was entering the Kingdom of God ahead of the sacred world? Prostitutes before preachers? Tax collectors before theologians? Lousy sinners before us? He must be kidding.

But it seems that Jesus wasn't smiling.

The good feeling was long gone.

It seems that to Jesus the construct of forms was not that helpful. In fact in some cases, it would seem that the forms that have been developed for the "sacred", Jesus considered to be a liability rather than a benefit to the Kingdom of God.

Jesus' teachings of the Kingdom, more often than not, were contrasted against what was commonly thought of as sacred. Scandalous from the perspective of the pious. Gracious from the perspective of the spiritually needy.

FORM SURVIVORS

It's easy to pick on the first century Pharisees; they are a really easy target for twenty-first century evangelicals. We have the benefit of reading about them in some of their poorest showings. Peering into the Gospels can sometimes feel like the very first edition of a reality show. Survivor: Judea. Pharisees trying to outplay, outwit and outlast Jesus. The lens of the Gospels catches the Pharisees in some of their worst moments. They seem to be voted off the scene, one episode at a time, until now they are just a funny little memory.

Poor, pathetic Pharisees.

But before we get too smug in our twenty-first century evangelical sophistication, let's consider that perhaps the lessons learned by the Pharisees still have universal application. Forms of sacred and secular help us in building world-class religions, but they are of very little help in following Jesus.

It wasn't only the pious that had to learn this lesson.

In John 4, Jesus has a sacred/secular form discussion with someone on the other side of the spectrum from the religious right: an unseemly woman whose life seemed to be totally out of control. We remember her as The Woman at the Well.

We all know the story. Jesus sends His disciples off to buy food. He waits by a well, resting from His walk from Judea en route to Galilee. While He waits, a woman approaches to draw water. Not a rare occurrence, except that this woman was avoiding someone—actually everyone. She came in the midst of the blistering heat, instead of coming, like everyone else, in the cool morning. Jesus knew straightaway that this was a woman who needed to experience His grace.

Jesus asked for a drink. From most men this would sound like a pick-up line to this over-experienced woman. But it didn't sound that way coming from Jesus. She was curious.

"Why would this righteous man talk with the likes of me?" she may have thought to herself. Whatever she was thinking about the nature of Jesus' persona, she didn't let on. She played it cool and went straight into a sacred form discussion.

You are a Jew and I am a Samaritan woman. How can you ask me for a drink? (For Jews do not associate with Samaritans.) (John 4:9)

There were rules about these sorts of things. Sacred rules. Jews don't talk to Samaritans. Jewish men certainly do not talk with Samaritan women.

Jesus then spoke about water. Special living water that is a once-for-all drink. "No more trips up to the well in this sweltering heat?" she pondered to herself. "Sounds far-fetched, but this fellow, there's something about Him . . ."

Convinced that Jesus could deliver the goods, she asked for a generous helping of this miracle elixir. She couldn't help but think, "No more trips up the hill. No more sunburns. I can stay home and lay low and forget about this stinking world! No more putting up with . . ."

Jesus interrupted her euphoric celebration with seven crushing words:

Go, call your husband and come back. (John 4:16)

"Outed!" she thought. "I knew that this was too good to be true. There's always fine print. A girl like me can never catch a break." She offered some token resistance, but she knew that her secret was not a secret anywhere. "This man must have known why I was here in the scorching sun. No more pretending that I'm Mrs. Homemaker."

But then in one last valiant attempt to conceal her shame, she offered weakly:

"I have no husband." (John 4:17)

"Maybe he will buy that," she thought. "Perhaps He'll drop it and I'll never have to reveal my sordid past. It's none of His business anyway. That will be the day that I'll tell this pompous Jew my story. 'Go, call your husband!' Who does He think He is anyway?" But before she could gather her emotions into one coherent sentence, Jesus said:

"You are right when you say you have no husband. The fact is, you have had five husbands, and the man you now have is not your husband. What you have just said is quite true." John 4:17-18

And with that, her indignant spirit turned into resignation. The fire left her eyes, her shoulders drooped forward, her head hung down and she lifelessly plopped herself down on the ground. "Does everybody know? Do strangers even know? Is it that obvious? Is 'whore' written across my face?"

And then she began to think more clearly. "How could this stranger have known? It wouldn't take a Jerusalem Scholar to figure out that I am . . . well . . . relationally challenged. But how did He know about Ben and Alph and Lukey and Nate and Joey and even . . . Sammy? Nobody knows about Sammy. This is more than just rational deduction. This man knows me. But how?"

Her questions came out as an observation:

"Sir," the woman said, "I can see that you are a prophet." (John 4:19)

"That was safe," she thought. "Prophet. Perfect. Now to turn the focus off of Sammy and me. Let's talk religious controversy. He'll love it. Everyone knows that prophets love religious controversies." And so the woman picked herself up off the ground, dusted herself, and with every ounce of energy that she could muster, she looked Jesus straight in the eyes and said:

"Our fathers worshiped on this mountain, but you Jews claim that the place where we must worship is in Jerusalem." John 4:20

As the words streamed out of her mouth, her feelings of guilt seemed to be again replaced with those familiar feelings of indignation. "Who was this Jew to come into our region and talk to me about Sammy? They can't even get their own religion right. What's so holy about their stupid Jerusalem anyway? Our fathers never worshipped in Jerusalem—they worshipped right here in good old Samaria. Does this guy think He's better than Abraham? Of all the nerve!"

This felt much better to the woman. No longer were they talking about sin and Sammy. Now they were talking about the important stuff. Big picture sacred stuff. "Which of our sacred forms was the right one?" was at the heart of what the woman wanted the prophet to answer.

It wasn't that Jesus couldn't spot a smokescreen that caused Him to take the woman's evasion bait. Jesus was, once again, two steps ahead. The issue really wasn't Sammy and the string of broken relationships that preceded him. Nor was it mountains and proper places of worship. Those were all outward symptoms of a far deeper brokenness. The issue was spiritual honesty. Jesus, without a moment's hesitation, declared with the authority that only could come from His position in the Godhead:

"Believe me, woman, a time is coming when you will worship the Father neither on this mountain nor in Jerusalem. You Samaritans worship what you do not know; we worship what we do know, for salvation is from the Jews. Yet a time is coming and has now come when the true worshipers will worship the Father in spirit and truth, for they are the kind of worshipers the Father seeks. God is

spirit, and His worshipers must worship in spirit and in truth."
(John 4:21-2

What was Jesus saying? Were the Jewish people right? Were
the Samaritan people right? Were they both right? Neither right?
What was Jesus saying about our forms?

It seems that Jesus was teaching that authentic spirituality is
not found in our sacred forms. Authentic spirituality is found only
when God's people worship Him "in spirit and in truth." Sacred
forms can occasionally become a vehicle for authentic worship,
but they can never replace it. Forms such as cathedrals and choirs
and praise bands and altar-calls and deep, insightful, passionate
expository sermons may assist us in the process of worship, but
they can never replace a heart of worship. The Father seeks wor-
shippers who are spiritually honest. Men and women and children who open their lives up to Him for complete access—with
no sacred/secular divisions. The distinctions of the sacred and the
secular were not spiritual compartments that Jesus ever acknowledged as valid. Jesus navigated through both of these man-made
categories in spirit and in truth.

History has demonstrated to all who want
to see that what is done in the name of the
sacred is not necessarily sacred. Sometimes
it is very evil. Conversely, what is done
under a secular banner is not always secular.
Sometimes it is Light.

If we have to have constructs, perhaps better ones than sacred
and secular would be "what is spirit and truth," and "what is fleshly and untrue?" Spirit and truth bring about internal transformation. We recognize our deficiencies and our complete inadequacy

to make reparations. The truth is we are bankrupt. The knowledge of our personal bankruptcy forces us to depend on the Spirit. In this transformation, by God's grace, an exchange takes place and we become what we lack (we become loving, or kind, or generous). Internal transformation "in spirit and in truth" is occurring even when sacred forms are not present.

We'll talk more about this later.

History has demonstrated to all who want to see that what is done in the name of the sacred is not necessarily sacred. Sometimes it is very evil. Conversely, what is done under a secular banner is not always secular. Sometimes it is Light.

SOURCES ALWAYS MATTER

		KINGDOM SOURCE	
		DOMINION OF DARKNESS	KINGDOM OF GOD
FORM	SACRED		
	SECULAR		

Many of us have been in enough Christian meetings to hear someone stand up and say to cheering masses, "I believe in the power of prayer! Amen?" And all the faithful dutifully respond, "Amen, brother. Amen."

Well most of the faithful.

Some of the faithful don't say "Amen" (or whatever the cultural equivalent is in your place of the planet). Some of the faithful in fact disagree with that "amen" rousing sentiment. I am one. You see, I don't believe in the power of prayer.

Before you slam the book shut, please read on.

Suppose that you were in the unfortunate position of needing one thousand dollars by midnight or you would have some prized possession repossessed. What would you do? One idea that you might explore is to make a short list of friends and family that you'll ask about a short-term loan. The thought comes, "I've helped out my cousin many times before; now that she's doing well, maybe I'll ask her."

You reach for the phone to call your cousin. She answers. You make several minutes of small talk. Now for the business, take a deep breath, and . . . "Say cuz, I'm in a bit of a jam. I was wondering if I could borrow a thousand dollars from you until next week?" She asks you a couple of probing questions and you answer as forthrightly as you can. Then she says, "No problem. I'll be driving past your place this evening anyway. Why don't I just drop the check off?"

After you had breathed a sigh of relief, you might think back to the process. Would there be any part of you that would think, "I'm so grateful for the telephone. Telephones work! I believe in the power of the telephone!"? Not likely. It is more probable that you would be grateful for the good relationship you had with your cousin and for her generosity. In this little fictitious example, mixing up channels and sources seems completely absurd.

Now let us return to the subject of prayer. Do we really believe in the power of prayer? If we do, we may come dangerously close to the life-extinguishing sin of idolatry. Prayer can become our golden calf, sacredly concealed and meticulously fashioned to meet our egocentric desires. It is possible to view prayer as a source, and thereby reduce God to the status of puppet, obligated by code to grant our every wish. (To see this source/form confusion being uncritically taught, watch a few minutes of sacred television and observe teachings that reduce our omnipotent God to the impotence of Aladdin's genie coerced to perform according to his platform-stomping master's demands.)

Prayer is a channel, not a source. I don't believe in the power of prayer. I believe in the power of our omnipotent God who spoke our universe into existence. I believe in a God who delights to listen and speak to His children. Prayer is a channel whereby God communicates to us and we to Him. Prayer doesn't change things; God changes things. Prayer doesn't work; God works. There is no power in prayer, but all power and authority in heaven and earth had been given to Jesus Christ, so we pray.

The difference may seem very subtle to some, but the principle applies across the board with dramatic implications in every form/source relationship. Some may say that they believe in the power of expository preaching to change people's lives. But does expository preaching have power as a Source? Or is expository preaching an effective channel to bring God's people before God's presence? Certainly it can be often observed in its idolatrous form, but never accompanied with God's power.

Forms can be helpful if used in their proper station, but if forms are given Source-like status, they become extremely toxic indeed.

KINGDOM SOURCES

The distinction between Kingdoms was the singular division Jesus employed to describe the attendance of good and evil—a demarcation that better explains the reality of our experience. The forms of sacred and secular become troubling when we experience darkness in the realm of the sacred and light in the territory of the secular.

At any given moment, the decisions that I make reflect the Kingdom source that is influencing me and expands the territory of that inspiring source. These Kingdom sources are in full force irrespective of the sacred/secular forms they occupy. James, apparently troubled by the darkness found within the local church, offers a colorful picture of this spiritual incongruence.

> *With the tongue we praise our Lord and Father, and with it we curse men, who have been made in God's likeness. Out of the same mouth come praise and cursing. My brothers, this should not be. Can both fresh water and salt water flow from the same spring?* (James 3:9-11)

The question posed by James is one worth careful consideration. Can fresh-water and salt-water flow from the same spring? The answer implied is astoundingly obvious. Fresh-water can only spring from a fresh water source. Salt-water may flow through many distinct channels, but it originates only from a salt-water source. They cannot be confused because they are two dissimilar fluids springing from two divergent sources.

The salinity of our thoughts, words and actions reveal their source.

What is the source of this dichotomy found even in our sacred forms? Positionally, I may have been transported from darkness into the Kingdom of Light, but functionally, as a Little Christ, I must relentlessly choose to make Light-like decisions moment by moment. James, with little mincing of words, explains the source-origins of the competing actions found within a local congregation.

> *Such "wisdom" does not come down from heaven but is earthly, unspiritual, of the devil. For where you have envy and selfish ambition, there you find disorder and every evil practice. But the wisdom that comes from heaven is first of all pure, then peace-loving, considerate, submissive, full of mercy and good fruit, impartial and sincere. Peacemakers who sow in peace raise a harvest of righteousness.* (James 3:15-18)

Despite the sacred/secular form that I occupy, my momentary actions speak with clarion certainty as to the Kingdom source that is influencing me. Attitudes of selfish ambitions come only from the dominion of darkness; salt-water from salt-water springs. Attitudes of peacemaking come only from the Kingdom of God; fresh-water from fresh-water springs.

From James' point of view, it just didn't seem that complicated. But, unfortunately, it does get more complicated.

THERE IS A "BOMB" IN GILEAD

Most of us would agree that obvious light and darkness come from sources of light and darkness. Truth comes from God. Lies come from Satan. Fruit is derived from its essence. That's easy. But everything isn't so cut and dried; subtle areas of dimness within the heart require greater skills in assessment, but are no less devastating to God's people.

In all our evangelical fervor, we have made a costly error in our theology; for many, we have reduced the cost of discipleship to a mere rehearsing of a magical prayer.

Even to its harshest critics, it has become obvious that the evangelical corner of the Kingdom has been growing in prominence and power. We now are recognized as a formidable lobby group with considerable influence. Politicians, from every camp, eagerly campaigning for office are now tripping over themselves to quote (or misquote) a Bible verse, knowing that this sacred act could endear them to the coveted evangelical machine. From the outside, it would appear to be a good time to be us. But all that glitters isn't gold.

In all our evangelical fervor, we have made a costly error in our theology; for many, we have reduced the cost of discipleship to a mere rehearsing of a magical prayer. Our evangelism has answered every question, removed every objection, and paved the way for an easy and quick conversion. Sadly, it has become so easy to be given the status of evangelical Christian that it can be done without ever experiencing a new birth. The process is essentially cultural; politicians have recognized and adapted to this new evangelicalism. And the evangelical subculture has flourished.

The essential distinguishing issue in this new evangelical culture is not the character of our hearts, but the vocabulary of our expression. Our subculture has developed universally understood code words that offer indisputable evidence of our club membership status. This is nothing new.

If we dig into our Biblical history, we will remember a clever military tactic between two warring kingdoms, Gilead and Ephraim, which has relevance to our understanding of sources. These two neighboring tribes were separated only by the Jordan River (take a peek at Judges 12:4-7). The people of Ephraim invaded the land of Gilead and were thoroughly routed by Gilead's superior leadership under Jephthah. Jephthah then organized his army to cut off every possible ford across the Jordan, thus trapping the invading marauders. A clear and decisive victory.

With the victory came a problem; there was a bomb in Gilead. The people of Ephraim looked, dressed and talked just like the people of Gilead; the enemy was now living among them and was virtually indistinguishable. The ramifications of this problem must not be overlooked; there can be no unity, peace, or significant advancement when the enemy lives amongst you.

Gilead was in big trouble.

To Gilead's credit, they were not content in resigning to the impossibility of the situation, but instead began to institute a clever plan to uncover the enemy aliens and diffuse their explosive potential. Even though the Ephraimites looked, dressed and talked just like those from Gilead, they were unaccustomed to using a 'sh' sound in words, but instead would prefer to use an 's' sound. This was the key to Gilead's plan. Every time a man would ask for permission to ford the Jordan River, they would be asked to use the word "shibboleth" (which means a fast flowing river) in a sentence. When someone would respond, "sibboleth", they would immediately know that this was an Ephraimite attempting to return to his homeland. Through this process, the Gileadites located and eradicated 42,000 enemies who were posing as their own people.

SHIBBOLETH, SIBBOLETH . . .

We evangelicals have our own "shibboleths," but unfortunately for us, they are rather easy to learn and repeat. They are found in our evangelical glossaries and come glibly off our lips; *fellowship, brother, born-again,* and *membership* indicate our club-status within the subculture. Use these words at the proper time with the right inflection, and brother, you are in! Amen.

To make it even easier to assimilate
into the evangelical subculture's social
conventions, we have gradually been aligning
ourselves with the greater cultures ideas
on materialism, pleasure-seeking and even
economic policies. Little change is now
required to become today's Little Christs.

Another "shibboleth" that is necessary to master is the one of social conventions. To be a member in good standing in our subculture it is necessary to share the same opinions on most disputable matters. If you show the same set of likes and dislikes (dislikes are definitely more significant), you can probably pass for one of us. To make it even easier to assimilate into the evangelical subculture's social conventions, we have gradually been aligning ourselves with the greater cultures ideas on materialism, pleasure-seeking and even economic policies. Little change is now required to become today's Little Christs.

The icing on the "shibboleth" cake, after the uniformity of vocabulary and opinion, is the ability to produce a worthy pedigree. If one can affect some civilities that reflect a godly heritage, such as consistent church attendance, tithing, and the occasional vocal prayer, it will comfortably ensconce unregenerate evangelicals in plush padded pews without anyone ever questioning the authenticity of his faith.

Passing the test of "shibboleth" is not difficult.

Jesus had a different "shibboleth." It wasn't vocabulary or opinion or pedigree; it was relational obedience. In His manifesto of Kingdom culture (the Sermon on the Mount), Jesus articulated in one short paragraph the difference between sacred forms and Kingdom sources.

> *"Not everyone who says to me, 'Lord, Lord,' will enter the kingdom of heaven, but only he who does the will of my Father who is in heaven. Many will say to me on that day, 'Lord, Lord, did we not prophesy in your name, and in your name drive out demons and perform many miracles?' Then I will tell them plainly, 'I never knew you. Away from me, you evildoers!'"* (Matthew 7:21-23)

Jesus holds up, as 'exhibit A,' an example of a spectacular profession of belief and testimony of sacred involvement, and yet who are a people completely unknown to Him. As we read Jesus' words, we scratch our heads in disbelief; this seems like a model statement, a beautiful confession. What's wrong with it? And therein lies the problem. There was nothing wrong with it. It was correct on every level. But correctness alone can never give us eternal life.

Sacred belief and practice apart from humble obedience to God's Kingdom-building revelation ensures no "shibboleth" before the Father. According to Jesus, sacred confessions and sacred practices without simple obedience to the Father, are only sacred to the dominion of darkness. Our confessions and sacred services are actually works of evildoing.

And so, we reconstruct our Kingdoms. Identifying forms is helpful in a few cases; understanding Sources is essential in all cases.

SEEING OURSELVES IN THE MATRIX

So, forms are forms. They are without power as a source, and neither inherently good or evil. To most of us, they come in two sizes: sacred and secular. Our religious instincts have been trained to think that the former is good and the latter is bad.

Our experience has taught us otherwise.

For instance, we have often walked into "the sacred bookstore," laid down our secular money and walked out with a sacred book. Our goal for purchasing this book was to increase our intimacy with the Father. But after reading, *"Our Best Life Right Now,"* or *"Living Life Without Any Limits,"* we feel less intimate with God and start to consider God as someone who owes us something. Unexpectedly, we found that this sacred form has taken us further away from faith. Has the Kingdom of God been expanded by the sacred form?

Conversely, you are driving down the freeway scanning the radio stations in your car. You come across a sacred radio station airing a worked-up preacher telling you that you're in financial debt because you haven't given to his sacred ministry. You keep scanning. The next station, KISS FM, is playing some sappy secular love song. You don't want to admit it, but you like this silly song. You're the only one in the car—so why not. You crank up the volume and let it waft over you. You're not trying to, but you find that all of your thoughts are being directed to your husband or wife. You remember all over again why, and how much, you love your precious spouse. That little tune seems to stick in your mind all day long and you find yourself being incredibly grateful to God that He has given you your mate. On your way home you stop and buy a single rose, or a T-bone steak, or whatever that special person appreciates. You arrive at home and sacrifice your needs in order to say, "Honey, I love you and am so grateful that God has put us on this journey together."

Which form advanced the purposes of the Kingdom of God, the special sacred book, or the sappy secular song?

THE RICH MIDDLE-AGED RULER

My adult life seems to have been centered on one all-consuming project: starting new communities of faith designed to reach and disciple non-religious people. This task seems always to require searching for three specific groups of people. First, discovering potential church planters who understand and are committed to starting a church with the DNA of reproduction and community transformation firmly rooted in its purpose. Second, mission-minded partner churches that will walk with a church planter for 3-5 years in playing, praying and paying (mission teams, faithful intercession, financial assistance). Third, we search for an appropriate core/launch team that will have credibility with the community we are trying to reach. These three searches can lead a person into some very interesting situations.

Over the years, God has given us favor with some tremendous partnering churches that have walked with us, in some cases, through the planting of a church, a daughter church, and a granddaughter churches. You cherish these kinds of partnering relationships. But, as in anything in life, discovering solid partnerships can be a trial and error process. Let me describe one of these.

I was invited to preach at a missions conference in a very large church with many, many resources. I accepted this invitation, in all transparency, with the hopes that it would generate a partnership for one of our new church planters.

I was picked up at the airport by the senior pastor in a leather wrapped white Escalade. He was a middle-aged gentleman in his later 50's who was indeed very gracious and warm. He ushered me into their brand new church building. It was jaw-droppingly beautiful. Everything was so tastefully decorated and fresh. Leather foyer seating, subtle flat-screen monitors positioned unobtrusively, wide airy gathering areas, a sloping balcony that wrapped around and hugged a very large, yet intimate worship center. It was impressive and very obvious that much time and care was taken in the planning of these facilities.

The missions conference was a one evening affair. There were four missionaries sharing. I was grateful to be given the preaching spot. The congregation began to straggle in—slower than I expected. When the music started the beautiful auditorium looked about one-third full. One faithful leader shared after another, each trying with varying degrees of success to convey the realities of their context to an audience that couldn't really imagine the reality of their situations.

Soon, my spot on the agenda was at hand. I really do not remember what my message was about, but as is my habit, I shared a number of what some people call "God stories." Stories of steps of faith originating from hearing God's revelation, seeing no means of physical provision, and seeing God become the sole source of provision.

And then it was over. We were warmly thanked, driven to the airport, and within a few hours, we were all back in our homes. "Rats!" I thought to myself. "I never even had an opportunity to talk about the possibilities of working together. Too bad."

A few weeks later, I received a phone call from that senior pastor inviting me to come and preach again. I was excited. It was obvious to me what God was doing. They must have prayerfully thought about all that they had heard and had sensed God's leadership to begin to explore a partnership with Toronto—North America's most unchurched English-speaking city. Yes!

Soon I found myself behind the pulpit of a packed auditorium. This wasn't a missions meeting. This was real church with all the bells and whistles. If you could not preach here, give it up. Everything led to the preaching moment with brilliance. Once again, I do not remember the subject of my message, but it must have been highly illustrated with more "God stories."

After some kind formalities with church leaders, I find myself in the well-appointed inner-office of the senior pastor. This is where I'd hoped we'd get down to the brass tacks of a church planting partnership. Perfect.

The pastor looked at me and said, "Jeff, you know all of those God stories that you shared these past two times?" "Yes," I said. He looked down and said, "I have been a pastor all of my adult life and I do not have one story like you told. Why do you suppose that is?"

This was not where I was expecting the conversation would go. Nor was this where I wanted the conversation to go. Any answer that I could give, any truth that I could tell, would not likely further this partnership process. My mind was searching for a soft, gracious answer that could redeem this situation and keep things moving forward. I couldn't find one.

"Pastor," I hesitatingly replied.

"You do not need God stories. You've got all of this," I said, gesturing to the wealth of amenities that surrounded us. "You have highly skilled and intelligent leaders. You can leverage all of this in a good business plan and continue to grow this church by ten percent per year. The only time that you need God stories is when you need God."

Okay, I had gone further than I had planned. *Maybe I can still salvage this by changing the subject to some of the many great things that this church was doing.*

Lead with a positive, lead with a positive . . .

"What does that mean?" the pastor asked in a humble tone. It caught me by surprise because I thought that I was already way too clear. He continued to look at me, as if he actually expected me to answer his question. "What do you mean that we don't need God here?" he again asked.

Okay, I was in now. In for a penny, in for a pound. No easy out. No side-stepping. No partnership salvaging tricky tactics to be employed. Answer this man as I think Jesus might answer him.

"Okay. Let's start with what we know," I began. "We know that people like you and me one day will give an account to King Jesus for all that He has entrusted us with. For pastors, I think that we can both agree, this would include the stewardship of finances and people that He has put in our care. One day, you and I will stand before Jesus and account for all the Kingdom potential that He has given us." Looking at the pastor, it was obvious that this was a thought that he didn't want to think about. Who does? It is not an easy image to hold in your mind.

"Knowing that this specific day is scheduled in our future," I continued, "Knowing that you will present an accounting for all the investments you have been given, should that sober thought not radically affect how you lead this congregation?"

"Just suppose," I continued, "suppose that you knew beyond a shadow of a doubt that God was asking you to sell this beautiful building, sell this land, sell all extraneous assets and give all the money to specific churches and worthy ministries locally and around the world.

"Suppose you knew that this step of obedience would mean that this one local church would shrink significantly in size, but the Kingdom of God would be multiplied one hundred times over because of this selfless investment.

"Suppose you knew beyond any reservation that this was exactly what God was asking of you, His under-shepherd. Would you be willing to give that kind of leadership? Because, I believe that until we can say 'yes' to a question like that, we will never have any God stories to tell, because we are not about His business."

Okay, I may have overshot.

There were no more questions. Actually, there was very little conversation. Needless to say, there was no new partnership to report. We both went away sad. (Mark 10:22-23)

Business as usual.

CHAPTER 5

THE KINGDOM OBSERVED
Four Quadrants of the Kingdom Matrix

Religion seems to value forms. Jesus stepped into one of history's most religious environments, and, other than criticizing those who were fascinated with the subject, largely ignored the discussion of forms altogether. Instead, Jesus zeroed in, like a heat-seeking missile, on the Kingdom Sources that inspire our actions of darkness or light.

When we position our familiar experience of the sacred and secular against the spiritual Sources that inspire the priorities within them, we find that we have four distinct quadrants.

These four quadrants can help explain the incongruities we encounter when we simply acknowledge the world of 'forms' apart from the spiritual 'sources' that motivate them.

		KINGDOM SOURCE	
		DOMINION OF DARKNESS	KINGDOM OF GOD
FORM	SACRED	**BRAND EXPANDERS** *...having a form of godliness but denying its power. Have nothing to do with them.* 2 Timothy 3:5	**KINGDOM EXPANDERS** *"The Kingdom of heaven is like yeast that a woman took and mixed into a large amount of flour until it worked through the dough."* Matthew 13:33
	SECULAR	**SELF-SEEKERS** *But mark this: There will be terrible times in the last days. People will be lovers of themselves, lovers of money, boastful, proud, abusive, disobedient to their parents, ungrateful, unholy, without love, unforgiving, slanderous, without self-control, brutal, not lovers of the good, treacherous, rash, conceited, lovers of pleasure rather than lovers of God.* 2 Timothy 3:1-4	**KINGDOM SEEKERS** *He has also set eternity in the hearts of men; yet they cannot fathom what God has done from beginning to end.* Ecclesiastes 3:11

1. THE SELF-SEEKER: *"A LOVER OF MYSELF"*

Where the dominion of darkness intersects with the secular, we will always find a narcissistic, self-absorbed person. This segment of any society, by virtue of their actions, unconsciously considers loving themselves as the greatest good. The Apostle Paul describes the condition in this quadrant:

"Lovers of themselves, lovers of money, boastful, proud, abusive, disobedient to their parents, ungrateful, unholy, without love, unforgiving, slanderous, without self-control, brutal, not lovers of the good, treacherous, rash, conceited, lovers of pleasure rather than lovers of God." (2 Timothy 3:1-4)

There is no question that the Self-Seeker has built a life on a house of cards. This fragile set of relationships and arrangements predictably comes crashing down when struck by natural consequences or by inevitable storms of life.

The syndication of *Seinfeld* gave us 169 television reruns that paint a picture of life in this quadrant. The creators of this series had a mantra that guided the development of this *show about nothing*: "No hugging, no growth." In other words, do not be vulnerable and never own any responsibility for the calamities of life. Week after week the characters of this series bumbled through a superficial existence repeating variations of similar relational errors without any self-awareness that they, themselves, might be the causes of the calamity. The series ends with the characters on trial because they were too self-absorbed to simply help a mugging victim. Numerous episodes flashbacked, one after another, as incontrovertible evidence that these characters were so ego-centric that they had little redeeming social value. With a sense of incredulity, the series ends with these four characters being shuffled off to prison, totally baffled as to why this was happening.

When thinking of "lostness," often a mental image of a *Seinfeld* character emerges in the minds of evangelicals. We think of someone whose primary motivation is "What's in it for me?" Someone who considers relationships as a utilitarian currency, unwittingly asking the question: "What will I get out of it?" Consequences arising from this life of self-absorption are usually met with a sense of incredulity—fists shaking toward the heavens as if to say, "I can't believe that this is happening to me!"

There is no question that the Self-Seeker has built a life on a house of cards. This fragile set of relationships and arrangements predictably comes crashing down when struck by natural consequences or by the inevitable storms of life.

We have little trouble imagining the Self-Seeker. Our pulpits have regularly constructed and denounced straw men who resemble him, because to many in the sacred space, he typifies all that is wrong with our culture.

Before we get too carried away in our self-righteous feelings of superiority, let's continue through the matrix . . .

2. THE BRAND EXPANDER: *"A LOVER OF MY TRUTH"*

Moving upward from secular to the sacred space, we find a second category entitled "The Brand-Expander." We understand from its dark positioning on the grid that we are to immediately disassociate ourselves from any consideration that we may share values with this shadowy domain. We are well trained from years of skillful religious instruction to correlate this sphere with either the Pharisees of old or with zealous legalistic fanatics found on the edges of our subculture.

Before we too quickly duck once again, let's take an honest look inward.

Has it ever bothered you that we see so little of God's palpable power and presence in our spiritual experience? The kind of spiritual activity that makes your heart race with a sense of holy awe because you have no other way to explain what you have just experienced other than "This is what God has done." The kind of things that so focuses your attention on the presence of God that there is not a nanosecond of fleshly appetite to somehow personally take the smallest portion of credit. The thought of your name associated with what just happened sounds ridiculous to you. There is no other credible explanation than "God has done this amazing thing."

So why do we see so little of this in our spiritual experience today?

It didn't seem to be uncommon to the experience of the Christ followers recorded in the Bible. We see example after example of the people of God obeying the voice of God and experiencing the power of God. The world had to face the reality that these "Little Christs" had an omnipotent authority that validated their message of Good News.

Conveniently for us, some have shrewdly constructed a handy *cessationist theology* that explains that God has changed the rules in His human engagement policies in our modern times. The really cool stuff was for an earlier time. Today, we have a more rational, cerebral experience with the Almighty.

Bummer for us.

If this new change of policy theology is in fact legitimate, why does it not sync with what we experience from time to time ourselves and with what seems to be normative experience in many places throughout the world where the Kingdom of God is rapidly expanding? Could it be that the teaching that explains our spiritual impotence might be more accurately found in places like 2 Timothy 3:5?

". . . having a form of godliness, but denying its power. Have nothing to do with them."

In the top-left quadrant called "The Brand Expander" we find a kind of sacred experience that is inspired by the self-saving impulses of the dominion of darkness and that has very few telltale signs associated with the presence and power of God.

When a brand takes on sacred clothes and stands on stilts in the front of the parade, there may be some darker issues to consider.

Why the term *"Brand-Expander?"* Brands are something we own; we trademark them; they become our exclusive property. We employ branding practices for three very practical reasons. First, they summarize, generally with a symbol, the culture and practices of our organization. They evoke immediate thoughts of carefully crafted identity. Second, brands are designed to appeal to loyalty. "I prefer this brand because . . ." is followed by some explanation of personal benefit experienced by the consumer (consumer is a significant demarcation in this quadrant). In a consumer-driven world, brand loyalty is an all-consuming drive. Finally, brands are how we keep score. The brand with the largest market share wins. It's a competitive dog-eat-dog rivalry designed to ensure that our brand is more top-of-mind than any of our opponents. The greatest good is to expand the brand farther and faster than any other organization.

Before I am too misunderstood, I do not believe that there is anything inherently dark about brands. Brands can be a useful tool in quickly ascribing characteristics or expected experience to the onlooker. But when a brand takes on sacred clothes and stands on stilts in the front of the parade, there may be some darker issues to consider.

In a syncretistic religious climate where democracy and freedom are proclaimed in our pulpits as biblical ideals, we easily adapt consumer-branding tactics as our method of church expansion. It fits our worldview perfectly. So, with evangelistic fervor we set about crafting our symbol, articulating reasons for loyalty, and subscribing as many as we can. Christian success or failure is at stake.

The compelling motivation of this quadrant is market-share.

With dominant market share as the goal, the Brand Expanders conduct a thorough and comprehensive analysis of their target audience. It is imperative that they know exactly what the consumer likes and what the consumer finds as distasteful. Emphasize what is positive, de-emphasize what is negative; it is not rocket science, but it is effective.

After the research is gathered, understood, and applied, an appeal is designed to zero in on the target group with military precision, by describing the benefits experienced when subscribing. The target group values success, creativity, personal service, brevity, and convenience. The same group finds authority, theological intolerance, personal sacrifice, and inconvenience as highly negative concepts—themes to be avoided with extreme prejudice.

In other cases the target values deep gospel-centric preaching, theological exactitude, and corporate achievement, while despising fluffy relevance, inconvenience, and corporate self-sacrifice. To expand this brand, ensure that one exclusively stakes out the high ground of doctrinal superiority while smothering any altruistic notions of corporate mission. It's a winning formula.

Fast-forward ten years. This machine has been running with peak efficiency, turning out benefit after benefit, subscribing consumer after wallowing consumer. Sufficient resources are gently pried from top-tier platinum subscribers to keep the membership benefits freely flowing. With all of our systems carefully tuned to deliver exactly what focus groups say our constituents require, how could anyone ever be dissatisfied in this Utopian Church? It would seem implausible.

Suppose this deep, provocative, unseemly question came to the consciousness of the occasional self-aware consumer. "So what?" "What difference does it make? What difference has this church made in my obedience to Christ? How has the geography around us benefited from the influence of this church? Why does it seem that church life is lived in its entirety on surface levels? Why do our facilities and programming scream that it is all about me—all about us? What is wrong with us?"

Who is the Brand-Expander? Anyone of us
who use the church of Jesus Christ to
insulate us from the expectations
of the Kingdom of God

That is a very difficult question for the Brand-Expander to either acknowledge or answer because it would require admission that the very basis of our community is entirely off center. For the Brand Expander, the greatest value is the brand itself. We interpret Scripture as it agrees with the central tenet of success and market share. We make an occasional reference to the Kingdom of God, but rarely consider that one day we will have a Matthew 25:31-46 appearance before the King Himself. After all of our deep expositional sermons and discipleship courses we find ourselves to be exactly what Paul described in an earlier iteration of our kind: *"having a form of godliness but denying its power . . . always learning but never able to acknowledge the truth."* 2 Timothy 3: 5, 7

Who is the Brand-Expander? Any one of us who uses the church of Jesus Christ to insulate us from the expectations of the Kingdom of God and ultimately from our personal accountability to its King. It is the sacred prejudice by the dominion of darkness.

3. THE KINGDOM SEEKER: *"A LOVER OF IDEALS"*

Moving across from the domain of the Self-Seeker, we find a secular sphere that, from time to time, is motivated by an altogether different Source.

For some of us, this is a new world.

Rick is a good friend of mine. He is an experienced Emergency Medical Services officer who has seen almost every kind of horrific motor vehicle accident imaginable. He approaches his work as if it were a calling, and his body bears the marks of working against time in some very precarious and desperate situations.

I first became acquainted with Rick through a mutual friend and found out that he was new to our community and enjoyed riding motorcycles. Since I ride motorcycles as well, I gave Rick a call, introduced myself, and suggested that we ride together sometime. We made plans to meet at a local coffee shop. That was the beginning of a new friendship.

I enjoyed Rick's company. I found him to be a caring man who deeply loved his family and easily became misty-eyed when speaking of the important things of life. He lived most of his life in the Toronto area and had a similar worldview as most Torontonians—that is, all spiritual paths lead to the same place. In Toronto, this is the natural conclusion that most people intuitively gather as they live surrounded by the vast array of cultures demonstrating devotion to the religions of their homelands. Although Rick had started attending our church, his theology was not yet Christian.

That being said, I began to notice that Rick's priorities seemed to more closely reflect the priorities of the Kingdom than did many of us who had attended church most of our lives. Injustices seemed to genuinely bother him. Catastrophic world events hit Rick in a deeper place than most other people. Even though Rick had seen so much misfortune, he had somehow maintained a very sensitive spirit. I soon realized that this was more than mere emotions.

On January 21, 2010, a 7.0 earthquake struck fifteen miles from Port-au-Prince, Haiti, at a depth of over eight miles. With this initial seismic shake and the subsequent 59 aftershocks, much of the nation of Haiti was left in total ruins. Thanks to 24-hour news coverage, we were all witnesses to this seemingly unparalleled destruction. Governments, mission agencies and NGOs began to cobble together relief efforts in order to bring some assistance to this desperate nation. Local church and community groups around the world began fundraisers to provide aid to Haiti. Canada, a deeply secular nation, gave more per capita to Haiti in those days than any other country. It seemed like every bank, grocery store and gas station in the country had some sort of strategy to raise cash for the needs of Haiti. Even the Canadian government had a program to match, dollar for dollar, donations given to Haiti. Money was flowing to the needs of Haiti.

This Haitian earthquake seemed to hit Rick harder than most. Giving money did not seem to be enough for him. He felt like he was being 'called' to go and personally make a difference. He contacted a relief organization that he was familiar with and asked what things they lacked. Crutches, prosthetic limbs and emergency medical supplies topped the list.

Rick made calls to every medical contact, called in every favor, and made appeals wherever he could to gather the precious provisions. He made arrangements with his family and his employers to take his two-week vacation immediately. He made numerous phone calls to somehow arrange a seat on a plane flying to Haiti. Soon Rick found himself inserted deep into the pain and carnage that the early responders faced in Haiti. His compassion and training helped, in a small way, to ease the suffering of some. He was where he needed to be. One more thing: Rick paid his own way.

Have you every wondered why those who we slate in the category of secular seem to have a more vigorous Kingdom pulse than many who have lived their entire lives under the banner of sacred?

Have you every wondered why those who we slate in the category of secular seem to have a more vigorous Kingdom pulse than many who have lived their entire lives under the banner of sacred? Has it ever bothered you that while much of the church is amusing itself into extinction, one conference at a time, secular non-profit groups are providing the muscle for Kingdom opportunities neglected by the church?

Most troubling of all: why is it not disquieting to Christian leaders that the pursuits that occupy much of our time, energy, and nearly all of our resources are seen as immature and self-serving to Kingdom Seekers like Rick?

What is a Kingdom Seeker? There is an impulse in God's highest creation, the one in whom He fashioned in His own image, for things eternal. Ecclesiastes 3:11 describes this spiritual phenomenon: *"He has also set eternity in the hearts of men; yet they cannot fathom what God has done from beginning to end."*

We yearn for our maker, but our broken, sinful state precludes any ability to be in relationship with the Holy and Eternal One. This exclusion, however, does not wipe away the eternal stamp of God's creation.

We understand that mankind has always been created for eternity. We understand that God is an honoring God; He will honor our living will for all eternity. If, while I live on earth, I choose to reject God's provision of salvation, then God will honor my choice in eternity, and I will live outside of any protection found in His presence. However, if, while I live on earth, I choose to live in submission to the Father through a love relationship made possible by Jesus Christ, then by God's grace and great mercy, I will live in eternity in the blessing of His presence because God will honor my choice of Him.

In either case, we have responded to the Eternal before we have any heavenly status made possible through justification.

Even in a fallen state, it is apparent to a casual observer that there are some who respond to the eternal things of the Kingdom before they ever bow their knee to its Kingly Source. They are almost like homing pigeons responding to impulses of truth wherever they can see it. Pre-wired by their Heavenly Creator, they instinctively recognize the absence of mercy and justice in human affairs and personally seek to be, in themselves, a remedy.

While the Brand-Expander chooses to value temporal effects that bring more comfort or prestige to its cardholding constituency, Kingdom Seekers believe that people are of paramount importance and will personally sacrifice for the bona fide needs that they discover. They look with suspicion at those who claim to speak for the Almighty but who live lives of perpetual unconcern with what any God of love should value. This persistent contradiction exemplified by Brand-Expander has fueled some of the wariness of Kingdom Seekers to become involved in something as inconsequential as organized religion. Who can blame them?

Somehow, those in this quadrant have squarely connected to Kingdom causes before they have connected to the King. (We will see later that the church that positions itself on God's Kingdom agenda will find that they will have a voice of credibility to interpret the Kingdom's Source to the listening ears of this audience.)

4. THE KINGDOM EXPANDER: *"A LOVER OF CHRIST"*

Dan was a pastor of a church that, until recent history, had a reputation as a 'mover and shaker' in the evangelical landscape of Toronto. Unfortunately some bad decisions and a successive parade of short-term pastorates left this congregation a shell of its former glory. An impressive building strategically located on a busy thoroughfare stood as a monument of what had once been.

Dan was called as senior pastor over a small staff of three (which included a secretary) with the hopes of 'righting the ship' and bringing back the glory years. As is often the case, the pastor search committee and the congregation never really listened to the message and heartbeat of their pastoral candidate; they just knew that they really needed to snag an impressive leader. Dan was their dream come true.

Dan began to prepare God's people for the mission that he had promised in earlier interviews with committees and elders and deacons and just about everyone else. For perhaps the first time in its history, this church was about to be on mission in its community. Over the next several years, skillfully crafted sermons were delivered Sunday after Sunday on themes familiar to this audience, yet somehow strangely unfamiliar as well. They were very accustomed to messages on the traditional evangelical underpinnings of missions and evangelism, but somehow these messages seemed uncomfortably different.

Missions and evangelism had always been subtly and carefully attached to the welfare of the church. Admittedly, evangelism was for some an easier pill to swallow, because evangelism paid the bills; missions meant lost revenue.

To others, however, the idea of missions was far more compelling because it could be accomplished without any personal risk. A simple check at Christmas or Easter eased the conscience like a magical elixir. Everybody got something good out of these historic themes. At least they used to.

Dan, the "dream come true" pastor, soon became a nightmare to those who most cherished the good ole days. Dan insisted with both the conviction of an evangelist and the focus of a missionary that their church should take spiritual responsibility for every man, woman and child in their immediate community. This meant that everyone in their community would have an opportunity to see and hear and taste and smell the Good News of Jesus Christ. What warm-blooded Christ-follower could argue with that? As an evangelical sentiment, almost nobody. As an executable objective, there were plenty.

Dan began to analyze his community of spiritual responsibility and found that his principally white, middle-class congregation did not at all reflect the demographics that surrounded them. If they were truly to bring the Good News to the ethnic and socio-economic diversity that ensconced them, they were going to need more than the one white, middle-classed fishhook. Through Dan's leadership, they were once again growing, but their growth did not entirely resemble their community. Additionally, their church was not touching any of the substantial social needs that encircled them. Dan instinctively knew that there was much work to be done.

He began to talk with his leadership about starting new congregations that would speak the heart language of the community. Their church building was more than adequate to house numerous congregations simultaneously. To the bean counters, he positioned it as a stewardship issue. To the missions people, it was world missions in their backyard. To the evangelism people, it was saturation sowing at its finest. To the mystics, it was Acts chapter two all over again. To the "white and uptight," it was reaching the biker-class that would never feel comfortable in their services. There was something for everyone here. Or was there?

At first blush, it seemed that Dan had struck upon a winning idea. But, as they say, the devil is in the details; many questions from significant stakeholders had yet to be answered. Questions like: "Who is going to pay for this endeavor (is this going to cost us more)? Won't this spread you too thin, Pastor?" "Will we have to serve more?" "How will we afford the upkeep?" "Won't these people wreck our building?" And then finally, the question behind all the other questions, "How will all of this help us grow our church?"

Pastor Dan, who had a huge heart for the Kingdom of God, had run face-first into the brick wall of church growth. His off-the-cuff answer of "all the good that we will be doing in the community should generate plenty of interest in our church and attract other Kingdom-minded people" seemed like a thinly-veiled afterthought. To the stakeholders, Dan's plan was not at all well thought out. There may have been a modicum of admiration for his intentions, but the silly plan would never see the light of day. Pastor Dan needed to join the elders in the real world. They had a church to think about.

Dan had a decision to make. God had placed deep inside his spirit a passion for the lost multitudes that he lived amongst. Everyday he saw the sadness, hopelessness, and desperation written on the faces of those with whom his church had no credibility. Even though in Acts-chapter-four-like fashion he was 'encouraged' to stop talking about this stuff, he felt like it was a question of obedience to God or to man.

With a deeply saddened heart, Dan tendered his resignation to the elders. The reasons were obvious. Dan, in good conscience, could not continue to be the under-shepherd of a flock essentially unconcerned with the mission of the Good Shepherd. It wasn't a question of pride; it was a question of allegiance.

As always in cases like this, nobody was happy. How could the elders explain Dan's departure? He was too mission-minded? He was too evangelistic? He was too concerned about the lost? Any way you try to spin it, the optics were terribly bad. There was some back-room scrambling to come up with a counter-offer that followed Covey's idea of being a win-win. Dan was presented with a proposal and request all in one. The proposal: "Don't leave." The request: "Give us more time to sit with the idea of being missional." Dan prayed through this and concluded that if these sentiments were genuine, it would be well worth his investment of more time. In a written statement to the elders, Dan prescribed the conditions of his continued leadership, which included initiating a first church plant within their community after twelve more months of congregational preparation.

One year later Dan called me and asked, "Would you be interested in having a conversation about starting a new church?" Another year's preparation had not adequately prepared the church to look outside its walls.

Today Dan is up to his ears in Kingdom activity. He planted a church-planting church in his community that looks a little different from most churches. They cancel worship services once a month and engage their community in all kinds of Kingdom initiatives. This new church plant also holds inexpensive (practically free of charge) sports camps aimed at the working poor. Normally, many of these children would be at home, unattended, while their parents held down numerous jobs. This year alone they had over 1000 children involved in sports and learning about the Good News of Jesus Christ.

Dan also is busy catalyzing new church plants throughout Toronto. This year alone he has been instrumental in starting five new congregations and has a faith goal of seeing 250 new communities of faith started in the Toronto area by the year 2020. The Kingdom of God is rapidly expanding through the obedience of Dan.

So, what can we learn about Kingdom expansion from people like Dan? It seems like whenever you bump into Christians like Dan (you will find them by looking in the places where you would expect to see Jesus), you find a leader who has managed to flesh out both the theory of Scripture and its practice.

They are not the type of leader whose ego thrives on heady academic argumentation divorced from any real life application. Nor are they the type of pragmatic leader who runs roughshod over clear biblical instruction in order to achieve his dubious ends.

The Kingdom-expanding leader lives his life with the unshakable conviction that the improbable ways of God are the only paths to accomplish the eternal purposes of God. It is the Christian life living out the full intention and expression of both Ephesians 2:8-10 and James 2:14-19. A life of both orthodoxy and orthopraxy.

Orthodoxy in isolation always degenerates to a lifeless debate among sterilized and unproductive leaders that dominate the catechistic territory of the Brand-Expander.

Orthodoxy comes from two little Greek words that together mean, "having the right opinion." Typically it is used to express the intellectual adherence to the well-researched accepted norms of faith. It is the common understanding of Scripture that has stood the test of time and serves as a defense against heresy. Orthodoxy is always a very good thing.

Or is it? Jesus' chief antagonists, the Pharisees, had cornered the market on orthodoxy. The Pharisees full-time vocation seemed to center on keeping the letter-of-the-law. But, according to Jesus, they neglected its intent altogether (see Matthew 23:23-24). They concentrated on the forms of faith and abandoned the life of faith. They were, in Jesus' words, "whitewashed tombs." Orthodoxy in isolation always degenerates to a lifeless debate among sterilized and unproductive leaders that dominate the catechistic territory of the Brand Expander. Orthodoxy in seclusion can be a very dangerous thing.

Orthopraxy comes again, from two little Greek words that together mean "right action" or "right activity." In the realm of the Kingdom of God, the Kingdom Expander understands that Truth is not a lifeless concept that is somehow contained in the pages of a systematic textbook of generally accepted orthodox opinion, but is in fact a Person (John 14:6). This Truth, Jesus Christ, is in fact the King of the Kingdom, the Head of the Church, and is marshaling faith-followers to accomplish His eternal redemptive purpose on earth. Implicit in orthopraxy, or "right action," is an obedient faith to the King of the Kingdom. There is no "right activity" removed from the obedience of faith. Hebrews 11:6 clearly says that "*without faith it is impossible to please God . . .*" Genuine orthopraxy is living out our orthodoxy by faith.

Some, however, head straight to orthopraxy without first going through the protective margins of orthodoxy. The Corinthian church serves for us as a sad example of this pragmatic tendency (1 Corinthians 5:1-5). The Corinthians, in their laudable efforts toward church growth, employed the dubious practices of tolerance and this is when things began to unravel. The tolerance of their sin invariably degenerated into the celebration of their sin. When the plumb line of God's Word was hidden, the intentions of God were nowhere to be found. Soon the church of Jesus Christ in Corinth resembled anything but her namesake.

The Kingdom-expander lives out his or her faith in the crosshairs of both orthodoxy and orthopraxy. The former without the latter is lifeless legalism. The latter without the former are presumptuous pursuits. Neither comes equipped with the life-giving power of God.

KINGDOM SOURCE		
DOMINION OF DARKNESS	**KINGDOM OF GOD**	
BRAND EXPANDERS	KINGDOM EXPANDERS	
orthodoxy *no orthopraxy*	*orthodoxy* *orthopraxy*	**SACRED** FAITH/WORKS
SELF-SEEKERS	KINGDOM SEEKERS	
no orthodoxy *no orthopraxy*	*no orthodoxy* *othropraxy*	**SECULAR** FAITH/WORKS

FORM

The church of Jesus Christ being led by the headship of Jesus Christ will always be about the work of Jesus Christ, that is, the physical expansion of His Reign. This church, which is motivated by its love for Christ, finds itself behaving in very Christlike ways. Self-protectionist instincts give way to more sacrificial impulses. The internal infatuations become a deep external compassion. Frightened religious consumers are transformed into fearless Kingdom commandos. Soon the landscape has changed. Darkness no longer dominates. The healing presence of Light is apparent to all. From the small beginnings of the obedience of faith comes a movement that penetrates well beyond the insulating walls of the church.

It is a movement that no one could ever confuse with religion. Witness the Kingdom of God.

ORTHOPEDIC BALANCE

Kingdom leadership isn't usually simple or easy. Sometimes it is incredibly difficult. Often it is one person standing alone resolutely determined to resist the baser demands of others in order to accomplish something with eternal significance. This kind of leadership looks beyond self-interest toward something greater—often at a great personal cost.

This kind of leader looks at the local church in a much different way—not as 'the goal,' but instead, as 'the vehicle' to the goal. What is the difference? Let me illustrate it this way:

As I write these words, I am sitting aboard an Airbus 320. I look out the window from 30,000 feet and I see the unremarkable landscape of Great Plains and a long silver and white wing. Although I cannot see it, I assume that there is a similar wing on the other side of the aluminum tube where I sit. Why can I assume this? Because, we seem to be flying without catastrophic incident. The question of which wing is more important is a question which implies zero understanding of simple flight theory. Two balanced wings are always necessary to carry passengers safely to their destination.

**If the destination is the Kingdom of God,
then the wings of the church must be
balanced with good works and Good News.**

If the destination is the Kingdom of God, then the wings of the church must be balanced with good works and Good News. James 2:14-20 leaves Christ followers with little wiggle-room on this question. Emphasis of one over the other leads to a social gospel or a lifeless religion disconnected from the values that Jesus Himself lived. The results of either are catastrophic to the Kingdom of God. Talking without walking usually leaves our world wondering how good our news actually is.

Good works verify; Good News clarifies. Left and right; both essential. Orthodoxy and orthopraxy working hand in glove.

Why should we serve our community if our studies show that the majority of those whom we bless will never darken the door of

127

our church? The answer is found on the pages of both Testaments and in the yearning spirits of a desperate world who desire to see the selfless Kingdom of God being advanced by His Church.

The leader of a church with these twin objectives squarely in his sights is a courageous leader indeed. He will resist those who have mistakenly associated the church as the Kingdom, and demand that this new entity 'preserve itself' and cease 'giving itself away' in order to meet the dark objective of security.

SECTION III

Acknowledging Our Influencers

So far, we have witnessed that the influences of darkness and Light emanating from their spiritual sources can have an immense impact on our sacred and secular forms. But what does that impact look like?

Specifically, how might these influences shape us?

Chapter six is designed to illustrate a single biblical principle as it lives and thrives in each of the four quadrants. The principle we will look at in some depth is that of money, because it gives us such great insight into our spiritual well being.

The following five chapters will take a brief snapshot of five other biblical principles and how they can be observed in the four quadrants.

THE MATRIX OF MONEY

KINGDOM SOURCE		
	DOMINION OF DARKNESS	KINGDOM OF GOD
SACRED MONEY	BRAND EXPANDERS *religious consumerism*	KINGDOM EXPANDERS *sacrificial giving away*
SECULAR MONEY	SELF-SEEKERS *materialism*	KINGDOM SEEKERS *spiritual reciprocity*
	KINGDOM PRINCIPLE	

FORM is indicated along the left axis.

*"Man must choose whether to be rich in things
or in the freedom to use them."* Ivan Illich

We've talked a lot about fables. Perhaps one of the most popular fables in our Western culture is centered on the issue of money. This myth has been handed down through oral tradition, from one generation to the next, until it has become the oracle of our culture. This manifesto is as follows: "Money is a neutral commodity. It is merely a currency for exchange. It has no power in itself for good or evil. All power for good or evil rests in its owner."

Sounds logical doesn't it? Sure it does. Money is just like a hammer; it can be used to build things or break things. It all depends on who is swinging.

The only problem with our manifesto is that it would seem that Jesus disagrees. He taught us that money was not at all a neutral, but had a power and a life all of its own. The god, Mammon, demanded worship, sacrifice, and allegiance.

"No servant can serve two masters. Either he will hate the one and love the other, or he will be devoted to the one and despise the other. You cannot serve both God and Money." (Luke 16:13)

As Kingdom-minded citizens we need to be very clear about this point. Mammon is not at all an innocuous, nonaligned, or neutral commodity. Mammon has chosen its side, and it is not with the Kingdom of God. The power of money, left unchecked, will always corrupt and destroy. Jesus spoke more about the influence of this deity more than any other single subject.

That kind of puts Kingdom Expanders in a tough spot. It would seem that the god Mammon is an inescapable evil in the routine of our daily lives. What are we to do? Withdraw from our commission of being salt and light and escape to some secluded monastery where Mammon's influence cannot be so easily observed? That would put quite a damper on our assignment of influence.

Fortunately for us, Jesus' pronouncement of Luke 16:13 is actually a summative statement of a parable that He used to teach His followers about the management of our possessions. There is context for us to understand this God and Mammon dichotomy.

"The master commended the dishonest manager because he had acted shrewdly. For the people of this world are more shrewd in dealing with their own kind than are the people of the light. I tell you, use worldly wealth to gain friends for yourselves, so that when it is gone, you will be welcomed into eternal dwellings." (Luke 16:8-9)

Jesus describes the people of the two Kingdoms: the shrewd, cunning, skillful people of the World who are well acquainted and adept with the ways of Mammon; and the ill-equipped and almost awkward people of the Light who seem to be blindly unaware of its ways. That observation resonates with most of us. We are all too familiar with the ways of the dog-eat-dog world, and we have often been witness to the unintentional mismanagement of God's resources in Kingdom work. Okay, we are tracking so far.

Now comes Jesus' punch. He instructs Kingdom Expanders to master the god Mammon and turn its power around on itself. Destroy this power with its own tainted weapon. Remember, these are not two equal Kingdoms; the dominion of darkness has no sustainable defense against Light. Jesus' instructions are to master the power of money by turning its influence around so that people will be brought into the eternal Kingdom of Light. This is done with the careful use and handling of the hazardous tool of darkness.

So our Kingdom posture then is to use the resources that God makes available to gain Kingdom friends. Jesus' teaching is that money is not a neutral commodity but has a corrupting influence by its very nature. Because darkness cannot comprehend Light, Light has the distinct advantage and should employ it in the assignment of influence. Something unclean is transformed into something holy.

This is the very nature of the Kingdom of God.

With desires to be a Kingdom Expander, my responsibility is to understand how I might properly use the resources God has put under my stewardship: both personal and corporate for His glorious purposes.

To that end, perhaps this matrix will be helpful.

MATERIALISM

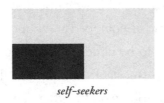

self-seekers

The darkest quadrant, the intersection of the dominion of darkness and the secular, we have characterized as, 'self seekers.' There are very few places where self-seekers thrive more than in the world of money. This is their territory. Home turf. The innate tendencies of money naturally pull the way of their ambitions.

> We live in a culture that uncomfortably is
> resigning to the fact that it will forever
> be a culture of materialism.

Let's face it—many of us struggle with the draw of materialism.

We live in a culture that uncomfortably is resigning to the fact that it will forever be a culture of materialism. Watch a Christmas movie from the 1960's and see the actors struggle against the forces that wish to commercialize Christmas. In the new millennium, the commercialization of Christmas is a given. The identity of "Christmas" is what is now up for grabs.

Who could argue that our Western society is anything but 'consumer' when we look at the vast disparity between the 'haves' and the 'have nots'? Inequalities in consumption are stark. Globally, the 20% of the world's people in the highest-income countries account for 86% of total private consumption expenditures

— the poorest 20% a minuscule 1.3%. More specifically, the richest 20%[‡]:

- Consume 45% of all meat and fish, the poorest fifth consume 5%
- Consume 58% of total energy, the poorest fifth consume less than 4%
- Have 74% of all telephone lines, the poorest fifth use 1.5%
- Consume 84% of all the world's paper, the poorest fifth consume 1.1%
- Own 87% of the world's vehicle fleet, the poorest fifth own less than 1%

Our very identity has changed as our population has shifted its priorities in its pursuit of materialism. We once held a noble designation describing our value as shareholders; we were once called citizens. Our new distinction relates solely to our value as materialists; now we are called consumers. From citizen to consumer. Surely by no one's definition can this be described as an upward evolution.

The levers of materialism on the self-seeker are designed to reinforce personal feelings of inadequacy.

The goal of the advertisers was to aggressively shape consumer desires and create value in commodities by imbuing them with the power to transform the consumer into a more desirable person.[§]

The lure of "consumer transformation" is at the heart of the lie promised by materialism. We are needy. The dominion of darkness offers an enticing solution to our lack of perceived self worth: "fake it!" "You are forty and you have accomplished some of your goals (maybe all of your goals) and you still feel completely empty?

---

‡*Human Development Report 1998 Overview, United Nations Development Programme (UNDP).* http://hdr.undp.org/en/reports/global/hdr1998/
§Richard Robbins, *Global Problems and the Culture of Capitalism*, (Allyn and Bacon, 1999), p. 15.

Certainly a red Porsche should solve the problem!" And so goes the sales pitch of darkness to all who will listen.

And so we pursue materialism with both arms fully extended. Nothing seems able to fill our insatiable hunger. There is no price too high to pay to worship the god Mammon. Sacrifice my family? I can always get another one. Sacrifice my health? You only live once; you got to make the most of it. He who dies with the most toys wins.

Really, this is nothing new . . .

"People who want to get rich fall into temptation and a trap and into many foolish and harmful desires that plunge men into ruin and destruction. For the love of money is a root of all kinds of evil. Some people, eager for money, have wandered from the faith and pierced themselves with many griefs." (1 Timothy 6:9-10)

When I'm firmly planted in the dark quadrant of Self-Seeker, I understand my only value to be that which I can personally attach to it. Because I resist the notion of a Creator, I am therefore responsible for my own identity, my own value.

Apart from a Creator, any value we ascribe
to ourselves is just a façade covering the
reality of our meaninglessness.

How valuable can I make myself? That is indeed a difficult question. Some have said that if you condense an average human being down to the value of its chemical components, we're worth approximately less than three dollars. We take our three dollars and put it on a $3000 cruise and we think we've increased our value. We take our three dollars and put it behind the wheel of a $90,000 car, and then we're styling. We take our three dollars and rattle around a million-dollar house and convince ourselves that we are indeed significant. We buy a two hundred dollar hat and put it on a ten-cent head and think that we've arrived. But the sad reality, apart from a Creator, any value we ascribe to ourselves is just a façade covering the reality of our meaninglessness.

Deep inside our spirit we all know that materialism offers no solutions, it just creates more problems.

RELIGIOUS CONSUMERISM

brand-expanders

What do you get when you cross the values of materialism with the subculture of Christendom? Self-seekers all polished up and assembled together in one massive brand expanding movement.

But this is not the church.

In John 6, Jesus was teaching the multitudes after a convincing demonstration of His authority. I wonder if some of His more pessimistic detractors might have thought that He was putting on a big show just for the perception of success? "Sure, feed five thousand people. Talk about a blatant effort of buying His followers! Can't anybody see through this? And then when Jesus did that water-walking trick. In reality, who beyond His own disciples actually saw it? Probably just another shameless "publicity stunt" they might have mused.

If anyone thought that Jesus' actions were solely designed to increase the bandwidth of His following, that objection was answered with one big, seeker-insensitive follower-reducing thud of a sermon. He said that being His follower meant more than catered hillside lunches and displays of the spectacular. Following Jesus meant, well, following Jesus. He said something about being "bread", and his followers were supposed to "eat His flesh".

His would-be followers were starting to get pretty confused.

To make matters worse, He ups the ante and says that any Spiritual influence from the one true God leads exclusively to Him. What's more, He dared to say that it was impossible to come to Him apart from God's personal influence. And the most audacious of them all was that He, Himself, would raise the dead on the big final day.

This Galilean?

"No one can come to Me unless the Father who sent Me draws him, and I will raise him up at the last day. It is written in the Prophets: 'They will all be taught by God.' Everyone who listens to the Father and learns from him comes to Me." (John 6:44-45)

Catered lunches and big productions were one thing. This was something altogether different. No carpenter turned miracle worker was worth having to listen to this kind of blaspheming rhetoric. And so the would-be followers of Jesus packed up their picnic baskets, dusted off their tunics, turned their backs to the Rabbi and walked away en masse.

Maybe the criticism that Jesus was all about an audience was unfounded?

At the very least, Jesus had a lot to learn about preaching.

Do you suppose that Jesus, in His humanity, felt the slightest twinge of discouragement? How about His disciples?

Perhaps looking at the dust rising in the air from the multitude hurrying to create distance from their radical teacher, Jesus turned, leveled his gaze at His disciples, and inquired,

"You do not want to leave too, do you?" Jesus asked the Twelve. (John 6:67)

Good question. That definitely was the elephant in the room. Surely that train-wreck of a disappointing sermon rattled even the hardy twelve. Maybe it was time to go fishing again? Certainly some time off to regroup and reconsider was in order. But before anybody could offer a ". . . well . . ." Peter's faith welled up inside him and he spontaneously blurted out one of the greatest statements of faith the Bible contains:

"Lord, to whom shall we go? You have the words of eternal life. We believe and know that You are the Holy One of God." (John 6:68-69)

For Peter, following Christ wasn't about the rush of the large crowds or the buzz he got from the momentum of everything going right. It wasn't about picnics and miracles and name-dropping. It wasn't even about walking on water. Peter had lived life and tasted the staleness of it. He wasn't a child anymore. He had tried life and found that it never delivered on its promises.

That is, until he was introduced to Jesus.

The answer to Jesus' question, at least from Peter's perspective, was, "Are you kidding? You have the words of Life. Until I met You, I had only known death words."

And then Peter gives the most astonishing statement, "You see, Jesus. We believed You, and after that, we came to know through experience that You are indeed Messiah!" For Peter, as it is with all of us, belief precedes experience. Trust precedes essence. Faith precedes substance. And therein lies the secret of the universe. Hidden from those who demand more. Revealed to those who walk toward Whom they have already received.

"The Kingdom of Heaven is like a picnic . . ."

Those who gathered for polite sermons and sandwiches and extravagant productions left emptier than they came. Jesus was a divine disappointment on a cosmic scale. But for the few that gathered to be near the One for whom their souls craved, there was no disappointment to be found. Jesus was bread and life and heaven all rolled into one beautiful Presence. There was no other place to turn.

So back to our original question: What do we get when we cross the values of materialism with the subculture of Christendom?

We don't get Peter.

We get the picnic crowd.

We get things that we often call churches (every one of us will see in less than one lifetime what Jesus will call them) that are set up and exclusively designed for the benefit of its club members, or for those who look and act a lot like its club members.

Rarely will you find servants at a picnic who find it an eternal honor to be used as a lowly table waiter if it meant that God's Kingdom is advanced.

We also don't find disciples like Stephen at the picnic (see Acts 6-7 for his testimony). Picnics don't need ministering candidates who are selected because they are wise and obviously empty of their own pride and are filled instead with God's Presence. Rarely will you find servants at a picnic who find it an eternal honor to be used as a lowly table waiter if it meant that God's Kingdom is advanced. Leaders whose lives are so transformed by the Christ they follow that they become self-selected as targets of persecution from the dominion of darkness. Leaders who could not conceive of trading their allegiance to their King for safe passage through trials do not hang out at religious picnics. Leaders who boldly declare what is not popular knowing full well the consequences that come pre-attached to their faithfulness have no time for our sacred distractions. Servants who, in the very face of all that hell can throw at them, offer Christ-like forgiveness to their persecutors aren't into playing biblical trivial pursuit.

We don't find disciples like Stephen in the picnic crowd. They have better places to be.

The picnic needs a different kind of disciple. A less zealous one. One who will be satisfied with quality sermons and quality music and quality parking. Or, perhaps one that can be rented with club member advantages such as fitness centers, cappuccino bars and mission trips to ski resorts. The picnic should always be exciting.

You might have noticed that it is exceedingly difficult to build something with eternal significance with the picnic crowd. The attitude of "me first" however subtly disguised as it may be, is like undiluted anthrax to the selfless culture of God's realm. We may be able to build religious theme parks. Possibly we may build some that come remarkably close to resembling a church. But we will never add one spiritual brick in the Kingdom of God when it is our interests that we seek first. Building the Kingdom of God and consuming religious goods and services are two opposing instincts. We give ourselves away or we save ourselves. Like the myth of the Third Kingdom, there is no middle ground.

As materialism has affected the very heart of our culture by changing our identity, so too religious consumerism has denigrated how we as church leaders see our constituency. Materialism has malformed citizens into consumers. We have inverted our expectations of people. We no longer expect people to contribute; we expect them to exploit. Talk of our "civic duty" seems to be a fuzzy black and white memory of a day long past. Civic duty is a romantic nonessential at best; what is now of paramount importance is our rights. It is only logical. How can we be helpful to society if we haven't received our fair share? So the rat race speeds up with every new opportunity to consume.

If materialism has created users, what has religious consumerism produced?

PEW PLAQUES AND CADILLACS

When is the last time you thought of yourself as a "saint?" In the early days of the Little Christ movement, that is how believers saw themselves. "Saint" carried the idea of being set apart for a very significant purpose—an eternal calling. The apostle Paul would write a letter to a congregation, the church of Ephesus for example, and launch it by saying,

> *To the saints in Ephesus, the faithful in Christ Jesus: Grace and peace to you from God our Father and the Lord Jesus Christ.* (Ephesians 1:1-2)

Paul addressed the people of God by the purpose that was implied in their spiritual status. Paul wanted these Little Christs to see themselves as distinct from their culture and ordained for the purposes of the Kingdom of God. Set apart and commissioned for the living and bringing of Good News. In the Kingdom of God, this calling, which is implicit in our designation of "saint", actually becomes our civic duty (that is, being remarkably set-apart from the consumer).

The days of saints seem to be gone. In the new subculture of religious consumerism, who wants a civic duty anyway? Today we have "card carriers" (how else will we know who has rights to the gym?) and "platinum members" (those who have access to the front of the line to for religious goods and services) and those who are "discount worthy" (those entitled to reduced rates at our brand's bookstores and schools). We have card carrying entitlement of the highest order.

Saints? That commission can come later. Right now we are needy. There is so much we need. Maybe after a few more concerts and conferences and trips to the Holy Land we'll be ready for the assignment of "saint."

Maybe.

Paul's new and improved epistle might read,

> *To the card carriers, platinum members, and the discount-worthy of North America; the entitled in Christendom: Goods and services to you from the benefits derived from our Christian brand.* (Delusions 1:1-2)

We have evolved from saints with callings to platinum members with privileges. Life is good at the picnic.

So let's return to the topic of Mammon. That which replaces our dependency upon God would fall under the category of Mammon. We can depend upon God or we can depend upon Mammon but we cannot depend upon both. Our fallen instincts naturally move toward Mammon because of our tendency toward self-preservation. Mammon is real; you can count it and measure it and put it in a big pile. You can depend on Mammon; as long as you got it, life seems pretty secure. And so we consolidate.

Is it possible that Mammon can be disguised in more spiritual clothes? Who was it that was offended by Jesus' teachings? The disciples who had left everything to follow Jesus or the religious teachers who kept everything to build their own following? Read the verse that follows the "two masters" discussion,

> *The Pharisees, who loved money, heard all this and were sneering at Jesus."* (Luke 16:14)

The teaching was hardly revolutionary to Jesus' disciples. They seemed to understand from the very first day that the call to follow Messiah was a call to leave Mammon. The deities were traveling in two opposite directions. Messiah called for generosity and self-sacrifice. Mammon called for consolidation and self-preservation. To the disciples, Jesus' call rang true. To the religious teachers,

Jesus' call was a threat to the very foundation of all that they were building. They loved Mammon.

They began to sneer to one another. "Sure, that's easy for this carpenter's son to say; he doesn't have any Mammon anyway. He probably wants ours." What they didn't realize is that this carpenter's son left the riches of heaven to give Himself away for their benefit. Their Mammon looked like a compost heap compared to the glorious splendor that Jesus had left behind.

The scoffing continued. "Sure we've got Mammon, but we do good with it. Our synagogues lack nothing and we tithe every penny to missions and . . ." Jesus interrupted their conversation of religious self-justification and said,

You are the ones who justify yourselves in the eyes of men, but God knows your hearts. What is highly valued among men is detestable in God's sight. (Luke 16:15)

"What is valued among men is detestable in God's sight." "What do you think the tradesman means?" They might have asked each other. "Is he against our sacred institutions? Is he against our religion?" They might have gasped

---

Jesus is not against our sacred institutions.
Jesus is against whatever we will not
leave behind to follow Him.

Jesus' words had pierced to their very hearts. They knew exactly what it was Jesus was saying.

And so do we.

Jesus is not against our sacred institutions. Jesus is against whatever we will not leave behind to follow Him. This becomes a testimony against our allegiance to Him. Whatever replaces our dependence on the Messiah is our god, Mammon.

Mammon can come dressed in many religious vestments: sacred funds, sacred buildings, sacred men of the cloth, sacred programs. None inherently evil but all potentially "detestable in God's sight." It all depends on where we point it.

If we point this Mammon toward ourselves and continue our patterns of religious consumerism and self-preservation, we fall straight into the trap of Mammon's power and we advance the dominion of darkness. If we master Mammon and direct it away from our own self-interests (and the darkness that is inspiring it) and selflessly use it to rescue friends from its treacherous grip, we in turn advance the Kingdom of God.

Jesus' warning seems to be one of caution directed toward our own tendencies of spiritually justifying our self-indulgent institutions. To Jesus, the Kingdom of Heaven is anything but a picnic. We have so many better things to do.

SPIRITUAL RECIPROCITY

kingdom-seekers

When we move down the matrix, from sacred to secular, and crossing over from darkness to light, we find a totally different attitude. These people, although not yet regenerate, find the accepted wisdom of the top left, the Brand-Expanders, as strangely bewildering. "How could that church on the corner spend all that money on a new stained glass worship center when children in Africa are dying from AIDS just because they can't afford medication?" They wonder aloud. Apparently not everyone finds our sacred edifices so attractive.

They operate with a different set of convictions: Karma

Karma is big. Many of our unchurched neighbors believe that the force generated by their actions will have some sort of ethical consequence in their life. Do something bad, and it comes back to us in some shape or form. Conversely, do something heroic or altruistic, and expect good things around the corner. Karma.

Interestingly enough, your neighbor didn't just describe karma; they actually described the Biblical principle of the law of the harvest. We reap what we sow. Spiritual reciprocity. The Bible is very clear about this idea both in Jesus' and the apostle Paul's teachings.

The Hindu concept of karma is actually very different. It speaks of a perpetual transmigration from one form of existence to another. Karma teaches of ethical consequences determining the nature of a person's next existence. Mess with karma and end up a dung beetle. I don't hear too many of my neighbors fretting about this.

So actually our unchurched friends and neighbors have more light than we give them credit for. In fact, if having light means acting rather than theorizing, then many of our unchurched neighbors may have more light than their club member cousins too preoccupied with brand-expansion to notice the brokenness of their community.

We'll have to forgive their lack of interest in joining our brand. Apparently they have better things to do too.

RESERVATIONS

As we have been stumbling our way in efforts to advance God's Kingdom, the King Himself has shown us something that is deep within the hearts of Kingdom Seekers—a spiritual desire to make a difference.

Jeff Hill, also known as "Bubba," has a heart as big as the north. As you will soon learn, that is an exceedingly large heart. Bubba Jeff discovered an opportunity to minister to the Cree First

Nations People in a very remote area of Northern Ontario. This reservation is located on an island with very little contact with outsiders. The social problems often associated with reserve life did not escape this isolated community. Almost every family has been directly touched by alcohol and drug abuse, sexual abuse and suicide. For so many, it is a hard and painful life.

The question that Jeff had to answer was "how could he help?" He began to ask a lot of questions, and with his questions, clarity began to come. He discovered that there seemed to be no shortage of money being brought in to help this community. Numerous government programs were available, all designed to bring some relief to the growing social dysfunctions that abound. What appeared to be missing in Jeff's estimation was the one thing that he was uniquely qualified to give. That one thing was love.

So, prayerful plans were put into place. Jeff discovered that the journey to this remote location required two stages of travel. First was a twenty-four hour drive from Toronto to Northwestern Ontario (the same distance as driving from Toronto to Miami). That is where the roads run out and the second stage begins—chartering a plane and flying over lakes and forest to this remote island community. Supplies and equipment would need to be trucked up and flown in several weeks beforehand.

The next phase of preparation would be to assemble and ready the first team for the purpose of bringing Jesus' love to the one hundred children of the island. Bubba Jeff began to assemble a team of senior high students and adult volunteers. The first year would involve a children's camp, and from that platform they would look to see what doors God might open.

What Jeff discovered in this process was something completely unexpected. From the most unlikely places he received, without ever asking, an incredibly high level of financial participation from the unchurched of our community. Strangers heard of the initiative and would volunteer to participate in fund raising efforts on behalf of the mission.

One such event that Jeff organized was called "Twenty Four on the Bus." Essentially, a twenty-four hour marathon where the team raises funds needed to hold this ministry. The bus was an antique British double-decker. The owner of the bus, upon hearing of the camp's purpose, refused to charge his usual rental fee.

Amanda, a young woman from our community, somehow heard about this effort and asked if she could join the fundraising marathon. We found out later that Amanda was a reporter—good press was to follow. Amanda would also start coming to church.

The Sanctuary, being a network of congregations meeting in sport centers, movie theaters, community centers, university lecture theaters, and schools, has no property of its own and no room for a bus. So Jeff contacted the management of a shopping center and told them of his dream. He asked if he would be able to park the bus on their parking lot. The management, in hearing the nature of the effort, not only granted bus-parking permission, but also pledged that they would personally match all the funds raised in this effort.

While Bubba Jeff, Amanda, and about thirty others hung out in the vintage bus, a stranger approached. A black SUV parked in front of the bus and its owner, a man in his early forties, jumped out and walked to the bus. He was curious and he wanted to know what was happening. Jeff, in his usual passion, explained their mission and its purpose. The stranger seemed sincerely impressed. He walked back to his SUV, spoke a few words, and then his wife handed her purse to him. A few minutes later, this stranger walked over and handed Jeff a check for one thousand dollars. He then told Jeff that he owned a trucking company and that he would ship all of the supplies to this remote village at his own expense. He continued to do this year after year.

Do you see the theme that we began to observe? God put a genuine need on the heart of Bubba Jeff. Jeff responded in obedience by taking steps of faith. Jeff's obedience was so attractive that those outside of the church began to take notice. Soon, Kingdom Seekers were coming out of the woodwork to be a part of this effort. We have found this pattern to be repeated again and again.

People outside of the community of faith respond with generosity when presented with genuine opportunities to help.

RESIDUAL WIRING

The Kingdom principle of selfless generosity can be seen in every community if we have eyes open to see. The fact that every person has been created in God's image is not a fact to be dismissed in the midst of our sermonic tirades on railing against the world. The thumbprint of the Creator has left such an indelible impression on mankind that humanity, some humanity, responds to with a sense of 'rightness' to opportunities for generosity. Motives may be mixed and intentions may not always be pure (who on this side of heaven is consistent in the purity of their motives?), but the affect of their actions is transforming.

Strategies for community transformation that involve Kingdom Seekers are incredible opportunities to bring Good News on two dimensions simultaneously. Communities are healed and the change agents may become eternally transformed in the process.

SACRIFICIAL 'GIVING AWAY'

kingdom-expanders

The brightest quadrant of the Kingdom Matrix is the category designated as Kingdom Expander. This is the space where the sacred and the Kingdom of God meet. When we look at the Kingdom teachings on resources, we see a radically different perspective on claims to ownership than we are accustomed.

EXPERIENCING "EXPERIENCING GOD"

Of all the things that we know, nothing is more assured than we are all accountable to God for the revelations He gives us of Himself and of His ways (see Romans 1). I understand this all too well.

No doubt, many who will read this book have read the bestseller by Henry Blackaby, entitled *Experiencing God*. In this book, Dr. Blackaby shared insights on how an individual or a congregation can ascertain and live out God's will and thereby carry out God's eternal, redemptive, Kingdom purpose. To illustrate this process, the author shared many personal examples taken from a period of history from the early 1970's to the early 1980's in the Canadian province of Saskatchewan. Dr. Blackaby (or Pastor Henry as he was then known), Jack Conner (who was my pastor and mentor for Kingdom ministry), Len Koster (a godly church planter who has since passed away) and others, exercised spiritual leadership that had a transforming effect on many communities.

If it is true that good leadership is about creating a desired culture, then Pastors Henry, Jack and Len were leaders in the purest form. They modeled the culture they desired. They modeled Jesus Christ. They sacrificed personally for this culture. And those who were caught up in their vortex thought that it was nothing strange. We thought that it was normal. We assumed that every pastor believed that advancing the Kingdom of God was their personal responsibility.

We had no idea at the time that we were surrounded by giants.

As a boy growing up in Saskatchewan during those days, I was a part of some kind of movement; I think that I understood that much. A church would be planted, and almost immediately others would be planted from it. Why not? There were towns all over the map with little or absolutely no gospel witness. Once in a while, someone might have said, "But we're not strong enough!", but I don't remember those voices. Instead, I remember the Kingdom example of "giving ourselves away" speaking much more loudly than the whiny squeaks for consolidation.

And so, in the most unlikely place, in the middle of the cold Canadian prairie, a warm wind of God's Spirit blew. New congregations were started without thought of the toll it might have on its mother's sustainability index. It was normal for young men and women to sense God's call to Kingdom advancement and throw their lives in, kamikaze style as it may have looked, with their Kingdom leaders. It was normal to give yourself away. It was normal to be concerned for the welfare of other congregations and to encourage them however you could. It was normal to cooperate together to advance the Kingdom. It was normal to speak of the Kingdom. It was normal for churches to give away their very best and brightest.

It was normal to walk by faith and it was normal to experience miracle after miracle of God's sustaining grace.

I had no idea that when I would move away from this Kingdom culture to attend university, that I would never see normal again.

There was a new normal out there that I had never experienced before. It was a different kind of culture. One that was far more sophisticated than the folksy charm I knew. It was more business-like. Church budgets projected with chilling accuracy the next year's income and expenses. I had never seen that before. Line items for missions and outreach were not the largest expense; in fact, they were one of the smallest. I had never seen that before either. Pastors would negotiate salary packages? Congregations would entice pastors to their team with monetary motivations? That was new to me. And even stranger than this was watching pastors consistently hear God's call to bigger and bigger congregations. Talk about coincidences. My backwoods experience of watching my leaders was just the opposite; it seemed that they would leave 'safe' for someone else.

> And maybe the strangest 'normal' of them all
> was that churches saw other churches, not as
> brothers in arms, but as the actual source of
> competition. The battle wasn't against
> the dominion of darkness; it was for
> our share of the Christian pie.

And maybe the strangest 'normal' of them all was that churches saw other churches, not as brothers in arms, but as the actual source of competition. The battle wasn't against the dominion of darkness; it was for our share of the Christian pie.

Church began to become a disheartening place for me. It certainly didn't feel like a movement anymore. Nobody seemed to be making bold steps of sacrificial faith. Everything was measured. Everything seemed predictable. Passages of Scripture that I had grown up on as 'staples of the faith' were now glossed over or explained away:

All the believers were one in heart and mind. No one claimed that any of his possessions was his own, but they shared everything they had. With great power the apostles continued to testify to the resurrection of the Lord Jesus, and much grace was upon them all. There were no needy persons among them. For from time to time those who owned lands or houses sold them, brought the money from the

*sales and put it at the apostles' feet, and it was distributed to any-
one as he had need.* (Acts 4:32-34)

While attending university in Missouri, I even heard one
pastor say from his pulpit one Sunday, "That's why the Jerusalem
church was in such need during the Judean famine we read about
in Acts. They had given away their base. They gave away everything and now they had to depend on welfare from others."

What was this? Barnabas' sacrifice created a welfare state?
This was indeed a new kind of Christianity for me.

I wasn't too sure that I liked the new normal.

I didn't know it then but I do know it now that, God, in His
grace, let me see a picture of what His Kingdom looks like.

And once you have seen, you are made responsible.

Sometimes a light surprises

The spiritual instinct of sacrificially giving yourself away isn't
relegated to the status of a warm memory only to be found in the
history books. The Holy Spirit continues to whisper this Kingdom principle to Little Christs wherever they may be found.

When our little band was about to start The Sanctuary, we
moved into a friend's house, (to establish this first edition of what
was to become an often repeated arrangement by necessity which
we lovingly named "hippie communes"), we began the task of
learning the culture of our community. Part of our assignment
included understanding the spiritual pulse of the city by visiting
local churches in the area. In one case, this was an exceedingly
encouraging assignment.

We visited a church called Chartwell, Mississauga; it was a
relatively new congregation that was meeting in a high school
gymnasium. It was a church plant with warm, generous heart,
largely reflective of its gentle and quiet spirited pastor, Peter Roebbelen. We gained a great appreciation for this man and this congregation. No vibrato, no positioning of image; you had the real

sense that through Peter's leadership, this community of faith was pursuing the very heart of God.

Peter Roebbelen called one day and asked if I was able to go for lunch with him. "Are you kidding", I thought, "any excuse for some personal space away from the overcrowded townhouse is always welcomed!" So we made arrangements to meet at an Italian restaurant the following noon.

The next day at the restaurant I was greeted by Peter's warm smile. I had only had a couple of conversations with him at this point, but God's presence in this man's life was abundantly evident. Peter asked many insightful questions as to our plans; he seemed genuinely interested. Not the kind of interest that you sometimes feel, like, "I want to understand how much of a threat you're going to become," but genuine interest in our welfare and our vision.

The time we spent was sweet. It was like one of those times that you sometimes have when you know that you have just found a friend. And then, over pasta and salad, Peter made two gestures that I was completely unprepared for. First of all, Peter asked, "I wonder if you and Jim and Garry would feel comfortable in serving communion at Chartwell next Sunday? We have sensed a bond and would like you to share in our ministry." This was an amazing honor to me and I knew it would be to the rest of the team as well. I accepted and thanked him for honoring us by allowing us to serve them in this way.

The waiter brought the bill and Peter insisted that he would pick up the check. As we were putting our coats on, Peter handed me an envelope. "This is just something that we wanted to share with you. We want to bless you and be a small part of God's work through you." I opened the envelope and read a very kind letter and found a check for three thousand dollars.

Peter Roebbelen and the people of Chartwell Mississauga didn't see us as interlopers or intruders or competition to vanquish. Instead, they seem to see us as coworkers in the Kingdom. We were planting a church in their "turf" and they blessed us. They were not interested in guarding their slice of the Christian pie; they gave themselves away, and in the process, they gained friends who understood a little better what it means to live in the Kingdom of Light.

I learned a lot from Peter that day. I continue to. Peter Roebbelen and the Chartwell church family have become heroes in the faith to me. We may have been of different denominations but we were not of different Kingdoms. Living in the Kingdom of God means that we are consciously living our lives in the very presence of the same King. Jesus' prayer in John 17 for "oneness" is only answered when His church gives itself away to build one Kingdom.

The *oneness* of Jesus' prayer recorded in John 17 found new expression in the seven years following that shared dinner with Peter Roebbelen. Peter and I became great faith friends, praying together and learning from one another's experiences in the venture of planting multiple congregations in the Toronto area. We had no idea that God was preparing relationships of trust that would greatly impact both of our futures.

Seven years later (this is a God story in itself), through two very different series of events, Peter was installed as the senior pastor of The Sanctuary, Oakville, with the presence and blessing of the staff and elders of Chartwell, while I concentrated my energies on the catalytic assignment of leading church planting in Canada.

A NEW MACEDONIAN VISION

When it comes to resources, the distinguishing characteristic between the Brand-Expander (top left) and Kingdom-seeker (bottom right) is *focus:* internal or external. Those who see themselves as essential to God's redemptive plan usually cannot resist the temptation of power, and use their resources to consolidate a kingdom constructed in their own image for their own honor. Brands are expanded as resources are strategically managed for maximum corporate affect.

The Kingdom-seeker seems universally unimpressed with this internal kingdom building. They see staggering needs around them and wonder why the church seems so self-consumed. They give resources, independently from the body of Christ, to help participate in solving the problems of injustice.

The distinguishing characteristic between Kingdom-seeker (bottom right) and Kingdom Expander (top right) is one of *process*. Kingdom Seekers respond to a God-given, innate impulse to use their resources to bless others. This truly is an action motivated by the Kingdom of Light. However, this action, as spiritual as it is, comes with predefined limits. The motivation is spiritual, but the power to execute this action is human. A Kingdom-seeker, as well-intentioned as he or she may be, has only their own human willpower to induce personal action (and we all know that our best intentions often get sidelined by the overwhelming instincts for self-preservation).

Kingdom Expanders are operating within a completely different sphere of reality. They understand that the suggestions of 'limits' are ideas that contravene the theology and instructions of their King. They recall Jesus' teachings about mustard seeds and knew instinctively that Jesus was not issuing theoretical platitudes. Jesus' intentions for His followers were to conduct His business with His power and resources. The fact of Jesus' exclusive investment in twelve very ordinary men was His 'plan A,' and He had not developed a contingency 'plan B' is clear enough evidence to Kingdom Expanders that His ways are not our ways. The cultural expectation within God's Kingdom clearly links the resources God gives us with the mandate God gives us. This linkage makes necessary the lifelong, growing practice of walking by faith.

Giving ourselves away, without even an expectation of reciprocity, is the Kingdom way we are to use resources. Do you remember the Little Christs of Macedonia? Paul introduced them to the world in one defining sentence of paradox, "their extreme poverty welled up in rich generosity."

> *And now, brothers, we want you to know about the grace that God has given the Macedonian churches. Out of the most severe trial, their overflowing joy and their extreme poverty welled up in rich generosity. For I testify that they gave as much as they were able, and even beyond their ability. Entirely on their own, they urgently pleaded with us for the privilege of sharing in this service to the saints. And they did not do as we expected, but they gave themselves first to the Lord and then to us in keeping with God's will.*
> (2 Corinthians 8:1-5)

How can 'extreme poverty' and 'rich generosity' be used in the same description? We understand straightaway that we are not talking about the sphere of the physical. We are talking about a Spiritual intention being activated by the Spirit Himself. This is not the thinking of "we'll do last year's church budget plus five percent." This is, "Father, what do you want us to do?" and then making ourselves available to accomplish that will.

How can human beings go from the reality of 'extreme poverty' to the sacrificial actions of 'rich generosity' in one breath?

Verse five gives us the answer, ". . . *they gave themselves first to the Lord and then to us . . .*" The Little Christs of Macedonia made one spiritual decision that naturally set into motion all the others. They gave themselves away to Christ. Galatians 2:20 was more than a bumper sticker to this band of believers; they actually considered themselves 'crucified with Christ,' The intimacy of their relationship with Jesus impacted every other area of their lives. From their circumcised hearts flowed the fruit of a circumcised heart. They gave themselves away to God. With all allegiances surrendered, they then were empowered to give themselves away to the world.

How like God to use the poor to teach us about wealth.

THE POWER OF SEPTEMBER 10TH

On Sunday, September 9, 2001, two days before the hijacked jets slammed into the World Trade Center and the Pentagon, a new church called 'The Sanctuary' was launched. We were very excited about the dream that God gave us.

The next morning I gathered with Garry (our worship guy), and Jim (our numbers guy), and Barry (a good friend and host of our hippie commune), to discuss what we had learned from our first worship service.

In the midst of our discussion, Barry's cell phone rang. He excused himself and politely went into another room take the call. Ten minutes later, Barry reappeared, with a concerned look on his face. Apparently a church in our city was in a financial bind. If they didn't make a building payment of five thousand dollars by 5 pm, they would lose a very significant and strategic investment. This was disconcerting for we knew of this pastor's reputation, and had confidence that he was a great man of God.

I could see by the look on Jim and Garry's faces that they were thinking the same thing that I was. I asked Jim, "What do we have in the bank?" Jim didn't have to flip open his laptop. He said, "We have almost exactly five thousand dollars." We didn't have to talk anymore; we all knew instinctively what God requiring of us. After our meeting, Jim and Barry made some phone calls and then transferred all of our assets to our brothers and sisters account across the city.

The next Sunday, we gathered for worship service number two. I was launching our first message series called, "Changing for Good." I scrapped my planned message for this series because of the events of September 10th and 11th and began to look at the problem of evil and the power of Light. As I introduced the message, we displayed a picture on the school's auditorium screen of the pastor we had just helped. I began to tell the story of this incredible man and his congregation's unique mission. And then I told this brand new congregation that we had just given away everything that we had. Radical? Maybe. DNA setting? Absolutely.

And so the matrix of forms and sources plays itself out; resources regarded as a means for personal gratification, or seeing resources as a means to participate with God in His eternal agenda. Two completely different attitudes; not differentiated by the sacred-secular chasm, but by the cultural divide of Kingdoms.

CHAPTER 7

THE MATRIX OF ENERGY

KINGDOM SOURCE	
DOMINION OF DARKNESS	**KINGDOM OF GOD**
BRAND EXPANDERS	KINGDOM EXPANDERS
competition	*compassion*
SELF-SEEKERS	KINGDOM SEEKERS
ego	*good will*

FORM · SACRED ENERGY · SECULAR ENERGY

KINGDOM PRINCIPLE

As we readily observe in our day-to-day lives, there is a remarkable worldview difference in how similar people from similar backgrounds approach life. The way we have traditionally accounted for this dissimilarity is explained in our regularly rehearsed theories of *nature* verses *nurture*. Indeed, these hypotheses give us great insight in some dimensions of human behavior, but they fail to account for the transcendent forces that impact them. As followers of Christ, we understand that a biblical worldview answers this question by accounting for the spiritual forces of good and evil.

When we examined the Kingdom of God and resources, we noted that these spiritual forces have a profound impact on our practical decision making with regard to our finances. We also noted that good or evil influence was irrespective of the sacred/secular divide. It crossed both worlds leading to similar outcomes.

We looked at some depth as to how our financial actions betray the spiritual forces that lead them.

Now, we will take a much briefer examination of five further Kingdom principles, and how we can easily observe them in the Matrix. The Kingdom values that we will study are *energy* (how we are motivated), *community* (how we relate), *change* (how we grow), *love* (how we bless), and *authority* (how we obey).

The motivating force that generally propels my life forward is a pretty good indicator as to in which quadrant I spend the most time.

What it takes to motivate us speaks with pinpoint precision as to where our passions lie. Rick Warren hit upon this in the opening pages of his best-selling book, *The Purpose Drive Life*. He explained that by living our life's mission we discover tremendous energy by living the life for which we were eternally created. It seemed to make sense to a lot of people.

For Kingdom people, we are told that part of expanding Christ's Kingdom (and diminishing the territory of darkness) requires a systematic and unrelenting process of scrutinizing the spiritual source that instigates my energy. Paul spoke about this process when he wrote:

> *For though we live in the world, we do not wage war as the world does. The weapons we fight with are not the weapons of the world. On the contrary, they have divine power to demolish strongholds. We demolish arguments and every pretension that sets itself up against the knowledge of God, and we take captive every thought to make it obedient to Christ. (2 Corinthians 10:3-5)*

The motivating force that generally propels my life forward is a pretty good indicator as to in which quadrant I spend the most time.

self-seekers

1) EGO

When a life, by design, is meticulously constructed for the sole advantage of oneself, there is no higher motivation to be found than personal ego. This fragile existence is dependent on a superior performance relative to those that I am surrounded by. As long as whatever I am personally engaged in is gaining ground faster than my peers, my ego is well served. Ego simply motivates me to produce a better showing in life than those I generally associate with. Superior performance equals positive sense-of-self-strokes. A poor showing means diminished fervor.

Ego is a fickle and destructive master.

The self-seeker's energy source is usually in a perpetual state of crisis. He is an empty creature devoid of any vigor stemming from a spiritual allegiance; energy sources are very few and far between. When the highest good is self, the only propulsion that can intrinsically motivate is the empty pursuit of that highest good—the endless self-promotion of ego. It is a vicious circle. To feed the beast of ego becomes an insatiable preoccupation on an inevitably devastating trajectory. It is impossible to win.

There is always someone else with more, or better.

For the self-seeker, the inescapable energy crisis is simply a matter of time. Songs of regret will soon be played, but can provide little solace.

brand-expanders

2) COMPETITION

Not far from the sulfur stench where ego finds its origin, we find a similar motivator: the Brand-Expanders' all consuming sacred preoccupation with competition. It is really just ego on holy steroids and it's very easy to spot. Pastors and staff with clipboards and notebooks and three by five cards stuffed in their pockets wandering around the hallways consumed with the omni-significant year-over-year and year-to-date numbers. Will the shareholders be pleased with our performance? There is a lot to lose in this high stakes game of superchurch.

Shareholders can be a fickle and sometimes unappeasable master.

More important than these numbers, however, are some other numbers that happen to be totally out of our control. "How is the church across town doing? Bleeding people? Wow, that's too bad. We should pray for them. Wink, wink (I sure hope they head this way)." And we skip away hastily jotting down some happy notes on our well-worn scorecard.

As ego drives the self-seeker, so competition is the life-blood of the brand-expander. It comes dressed up with the funny glasses and rubber nosed disguise called a 'passion for evangelism', and then spends its resources on advertising on the sacred radio station to sacred prospects with the sacred appeal that we are the church with the deep and sacred teaching.

It talks like it has great interest in reaching the city while it skillfully maneuvers the ecclesiastical machinery to block any new churches from starting. "Why do we need another church in this town? Our second service is only half full and besides that, we are eleven percent behind budget. This town doesn't need another church, it will just dilute our market-share."

To ensure that nobody gets the crazy idea of starting a new sacred assembly in our community, we take a corporate page from the Fortune 500 company's playbook and require our pastoral teams to sign contracts with 'non competition' clauses. It just makes good business sense.

Why compete with ourselves?

However we dress it up, the impulse of competition in the sacred space does not originate in the heavenlies, and is in fact, an affront to the Kingdom of God.

However we dress it up, the impulse of competition in the sacred space does not originate in the heavenlies, and is in fact, an affront to the Kingdom of God.

kingdom-seekers

3) GOODWILL

Goodwill is an interesting concept because it means many things to many different people. Sometimes goodwill is used as a business concept to refer to the ability of a business to exert influence within a community without having to resort to the use of its capital. Other times it is used as an accounting term in the determination of a business' value that is not directly attributable to tangible assets and liabilities. This value derives from factors such as consumer loyalty to the brand. But most often we use this word in a less technical way that describes an altruistic motivation. This motivation may not be fully and purely selfless at all times, but at worst, selfish benefits are a byproduct of the action and not their driving intention.

As we examined earlier, there seems to be a fast-growing segment of our population that is deeply interested in correcting social injustices and meeting honest human needs. This preoccupation is not a new phenomenon—we can see a vivid example of this kind of Kingdom Seeker in the person of Cornelius:

> *"At Caesarea there was a man named Cornelius, a centurion of what was known as the Italian Cohort, a devout man who feared God with all his household, gave alms generously to the people . . ."*
> Acts 10:1-2 (ESV)

Was Cornelius a Spirit-filled Christ-follower at the time of this introduction? Negative. By Luke's description, he seems to well fit the moniker of a Kingdom-seeker. Cornelius was a man, who, before experiencing spiritual rebirth, had an impulse toward the King and His Kingdom. He feared God, prayed, and philanthropically met human needs out of his own financial resources. He had not yet been accurately introduced to the person of Christ, yet he seemed to prize Kingdom ideals.

Marching to the same drumbeat as Cornelius, we can easily see a long parade of people inspired to sacrifice time, energy and personal resources for the good of others. There is nothing materially 'in it' for these Kingdom Seekers who seem to be motivated by nothing more than an internal drive to bless.

The ill-conceived caricatures of the lost that authoritatively belch from lofty leaders in ivory towers who themselves have long ceased associating with those outside the club seem to portray the lost as universally deviant, depraved and debauched. Listen long enough to these demanding prophets and any potential Kingdom army winces in dread as it visualizes its evangelistic approach to a netherworld full of the degenerate descendants of Attila the Hun.

Maybe we won't bother with the lost. They don't seem to like us either.

But the straw men that are concocted and disseminated from the ivory tower do not really resemble the modern iterations of Cornelius that we can observe performing selfless acts of altruism. These observations create some problems for us. Do they really have an evil 'end' in mind for these generous 'means' that they offer? Does not one miniscule vestige of the Father's handiwork remain in these wretched beasts that we are called to evangelize? Why are they behaving so selflessly?

Confusing.

But maybe it shouldn't be. For the Kingdom-seeker, goodwill seems to be a motivating force of its own.

kingdom-expanders

4) COMPASSION

Throughout history, the world has been indelibly marked, both negatively and positively, by actions carried out in the name of Christ. Flipping through the tattered pages of antiquity reveals numerous tragic and horrific exploits bearing Jesus' distinguishing brand. Turning the crisp pages of today's newspapers reveals numerous similar, yet more refined assertions of human will in the name of Christ's will.

We have a long and storied tradition.

However, the history of mankind has also been eternally influenced by some of the least likely heroes. Men and women who never sought the spotlight, and in most cases, who were never honored by their contemporaries. People who were moved with compassion at the great need they had observed. That observation, unshakably locked in their minds, made them responsible. They could not, with spiritual integrity, turn their backs on what they had seen.

Okay, we understand this. These are similar to the impulses that we often see lived out in Kingdom Seekers. But what potential world changing, history-making energy source does the Kingdom Expander have exclusive access to? That is a great question.

Do you remember the entrance exam that we will all be receiving on our first official day of eternity? We can prepare in advance by reading the back end of Matthew 25.

> *"Then the King will say to those on his right, 'Come, you who are blessed by my Father; take your inheritance, the kingdom prepared for you since the creation of the world. For I was hungry and you gave me something to eat, I was thirsty and you gave me something to drink, I was a stranger and you invited me in, I needed clothes and you clothed me, I was sick and you looked after me, I was in prison and you came to visit me.'*
>
> *"Then the righteous will answer him, 'Lord, when did we see you hungry and feed you, or thirsty and give you something to drink? When did we see you a stranger and invite you in, or needing clothes and clothe you? When did we see you sick or in prison and go to visit you?'*
>
> *"The King will reply, 'I tell you the truth, whatever you did for one of the least of these brothers of mine, you did for me.'"* (Matthew 25:34-40)

The course of history has been dramatically impacted because some simple Christ-followers were simply not sophisticated enough to rationalize into oblivion teachings like this as some obscure metaphor with little instructive value to the contemporary local church. Instead, orphanages opened, schools started, homeless were sheltered, prisoners were discipled, the hungry were fed, the sick were treated, slavery was abolished, and human beings all over the world were loved because Kingdom expanding Christ-followers throughout history believed that Jesus meant business.

The ethical condition of our communities was never intended by God to be a spiritual responsibility handed over to secular authorities (in order to allow the sacred to concentrate on more ethereal matters). Though, throughout history, many sacred institutions have reserved their compassion for worthy candidates, other churches have given themselves away with reckless abandon to the brokenness they have discovered. With the love of Christ energizing them, caring ministries are initiated by both large and tiny Kingdom expanding congregations that selflessly minister to the hungry, thirsty, lonely, naked, and imprisoned.

Certainly history can correctly point out the mars and blemishes originating from brand-expanding Christendom—that is a reality from which we cannot hide. But history's recording of the Christian faith was not entirely centered on the self-indulgent. Where else in history can we find big helpings of compassion, generously dished out? Where else can we find the selfless concern and care over society's unwanted and outcasts? The history of mankind has been eternally altered by the heroic faith of Kingdom people entirely following the instruction and example of their Kingdom's Sovereign. The compassionate Kingdom rapidly expands wherever the people of God live recklessly obedient to His voice.

History has borne witness of this as well.

Knowing that an entrance exam awaits us all can provide a certain degree of motivation, but not the sustaining, history changing energy source that we observe in these Kingdom-expanders we have all witnessed. Christian compassion provides spiritual direction but not the unrelenting spiritual propulsion necessary for Kingdom change. If compassion, spiritual obligation and fear are the sole propelling forces of our faith, we will never have the internal juice to live a life of unwavering commitment to our King.

Compassion, as an energy source, propels us exactly into the mission borne in the heart of God.

But before compassion can produce its Kingdom-expanding fruit, something has to change. And so we examine the next Kingdom principle that has the ability to sustain the motivating direction of our lives.

CHAPTER 8

THE MATRIX OF CHANGE

KINGDOM SOURCE	
DOMINION OF DARKNESS	**KINGDOM OF GOD**
BRAND EXPANDERS	KINGDOM EXPANDERS
conformation	*incarnation*
SELF-SEEKERS	KINGDOM SEEKERS
manipulation	*transformation*

FORM

SACRED CHANGE

SECULAR CHANGE

KINGDOM PRINCIPLE

If any one word can characterize the age we live in, it must be 'change.' Things that once seemed to be rock solid now seem to be in a writhing state of flux. Our work, family, sexuality, technologies, theology, ecclesiology, ethnic homogeny, and even climate stability seem to be searching for a new normal. Change is happening on many dimensions at an unprecedented rate. These changes are perceived as positive or negative depending on which side of the pendulum you've made camp.

Like it or not, change is coming. Elections are won or lost on this theme.

When we speak of change, we generally talk of the external modifications. We worry about the way things around us are becoming different and our personal abilities to cope. For many in the sacred space, change is not a soothing friend, but a manipulative enemy. That being said, change as a Kingdom principle does not primarily concern itself with the exteriors of life (politics), but with the internal, invisible, eternal substance of our lives (character).

When coming face-to-face with the necessity of inner transformation, we tend to react in completely different ways. It depends on the quadrant on which we spend our days.

self-seekers

1) MANIPULATION

For the Self-Seeker, internal change is nearly an impossible assignment. When life is lived on surface levels, the necessary exercise of introspection and honest self-evaluation is awkward and unfamiliar territory indeed. If the internal change is imposed from an outside force as a behavioral modifying threat, the self-seeker often complies with the lowest form of change: manipulation.

We see this played out in various forms as an everyday occurrence: a faithful and devastated wife discovers a cheating husband's secrets. In order to preserve this suddenly important institution, he is obliged to make vows, promises, and commitments to a newfound fidelity. The danger of the moment brought to the forefront of his mind all that might be lost. The threat of that reality compelled a surface-level, albeit deeply passionate confession.

He was now a changed man. But in substance, what had changed? He was found out, his station was threatened, and he appealed for mercy. None of these activities reveal an understanding of why he cheated. None speak of any reparations in the heart of a man who would so easily cast aside and humiliate his bride. None can prevent it from happening again.

There was much emotion and heart-felt sorrow, but was there change?

Manipulation is the lowest form of change. It's like plastic surgery of the soul. It is reordering the exterior facade without renovating the heart. But it is really all that we can do when we live life on the surface.

brand-expanders

2) CONFORMATION

Dictionaries define 'conformation' as, "the act of conforming; the act of producing conformity." It is actually a biochemistry term that describes the forces that produce spatial symmetry in a single atom. Designed pressure to produce a desired outcome. This biochemical relationship involves two essential players: the 'conformer', which creates the necessary culture; and the 'conformed', which acquiesces.

Life, at its most microscopic level, is often mirrored and multiplied in the oxygen-deprived land where Brand-Expanders roam free. It is a territory that prescribes beliefs and behaviors apart from the life-giving Source from which they originated. Cultures are carefully and meticulously designed to produce uniformity of belief and practice which benefits one all-important end user: the brand itself.

Internal transformation and its natural 'test-able' emanating influence of God's perfect realm is reduced to a more manageable mandate of 'believe and behave.'

Do not conform any longer to the pattern of this world, but be transformed by the renewing of your mind. Then you will be able to test and approve what God's will is—his good, pleasing and perfect will. (Romans 12:2)

As a social ethic, there is nothing wrong with 'believe and behave.' It may have its place beautifully inscribed on our courtrooms and classrooms and sacred restrooms. But as an agent of change, conformation only diagnoses the disease without providing a path to health.

We are told from our sacred institutions that to be Christlike is to act more loving, more kind, more patient. We readily agree, who can argue with that? So we believe and behave and go about doing our best in acting more loving, more kind, and more patient. By mid Sunday afternoon, after we have fought our way out of the sacred parking lot, waited for an eternity for our lunch with the sacred crowd at Cracker Barrel, and watched our favorite football team get pulverized by the enemy—we do not feel too loving or kind or patient. We feel irritable. We haven't even made it to Monday and our peppy Galatians 5:22-23 sermon has already worn off like the healthy sloshing of Old Spice we lathered on just before church.

Neither the old lifeless legalism of 'believe and behave,' nor the cool, funky, hipper versions of a more open-minded conformation can produce the inner change that advances the Kingdom of God an inch.

The only change we've experienced is a new and greater intensity of discouragement in the pit of our stomach.

But wait just a minute. Were we told to *act* more loving, or to *be* more loving? Are we to *act* more patient and kind, or *be* more patient and kind? Hmmm. The former seems like the work of human will. The latter sounds like the work of the Spirit. The former is conforming to the patterns of our brand. The latter is becoming transformed by the renewing of our minds.

Neither the old lifeless legalism of 'believe and behave,' nor the cool, funky, hipper versions of a more open-minded conformation can produce the inner change that advances the Kingdom of God an inch. We may be marching in a straight line, but we will be following a different Commander.

kingdom-seekers

3) TRANSFORMATION

Eric is a really, really smart man. He was born and raised in France and moved to North America where he finished his education. Eric has spent his entire career in one major multi-national corporation where his intelligence, personal charisma and integrity served him well as he advanced to senior levels of authority. I met Eric when he moved to Toronto to give leadership to this company's Canadian presence.

He is married to a godly wife and together they were raising two pretty little girls. They had a beautiful home in the suburbs and they opened it for Kingdom purposes. So open was their home that they even welcomed a new church planting family to live with them for several months until they could afford to find a house. Eric was also a humble servant. Our church met in a school, so Eric the executive was a member of one of our "body builders" teams that set up each week.

Everything on the outside looked good. And it was. Everything, except for one minor detail: Eric was not a Christ follower. He didn't even believe in God. Eric was an atheist. He wasn't an atheist in the Stephen Hawking sense where he had a cause to prove. But, from his growing years and his educational background, he could not bring together the reality of the presence of God. He didn't think that he was against God. He deeply loved his wife and respected her sincere faith, but the thought of his own faith just seemed too much like pretending to him.

Sunday after Sunday Eric sat under the Word of God, and together as a family, they made adjustments to their priorities and lifestyle as they saw the truth of Scripture being a blessing to their lives. He was involved in every community transformation project that our church invested in. He was an extremely busy businessman, yet Eric faithfully attended a weekly small group. He wasn't hypocritical; everyone in the small group knew of Eric's lack of faith and challenged his position with gentleness and respect. Eric, himself, asked, in a seeking posture, some zingers of questions that made everyone retrace their steps and rediscover the reasons for their theological positions.

We all loved Eric and we knew that he loved us.

One weekday evening he was gathered with his small group in a living room and they were having a study on the subject of prayer. At one point in the evening, Eric was unusually candid. He said, "I know that you believe that when you pray, that there is a God that listens and goes about changing things in response to that prayer. I believe that when you pray, by your believing you subconsciously orchestrate situations and events in the direction of your preference. When it happens, you say God answered your prayer."

The living room was strangely quiet. Eric had not been quite that open before. Tom, a friendly and warm man of Italian descent, seemed nonplused and spoke in his charming way. "So, Eric, do you love your job?" Eric said, "of course." Tom continued, "So, Eric, you love your job. You do not believe in God and you do not believe in prayer. Did I get that right?" "Well, yes, I guess so," replied Eric. "Okay," Tom said as if he had something up his sleeve. "Would it be okay if the rest of this room, who do believe in God, pray for the next two weeks that you lose your job? Would that be okay to you?" "No!" Eric exclaimed. But the idea behind the suggested scenario wasn't lost on him. Eric discovered that day that he had a little more faith than he was willing to admit. And we had renewed hope for Eric.

Eric continued for a number of months to be a part of our fellowship and contribute in every possible way. His lifestyle was being transformed into something very healthy as he applied the truths of Scripture to the substance of life. He loved the people of Christ and the people of Christ loved him. Yet, Eric was unregenerate.

As is often the case with business executives, headquarters had another promotion waiting for him back at the home office. To me, this was very bad news. I was certain that God was going to use these honest and healthy relationships to lead Eric to faith; and now the clock was ticking. Soon we found ourselves waving good-bye to dear friends with a double sense of regret; we knew that we would miss our friends and we knew that we missed our opportunity.

Well, life goes on. I prayed for Eric a lot at first. Soon there were other people more top of mind. We would hear from Eric from time to time and would cause me to breathe a prayer for his salvation. Soon, three years had passed when I received a phone call during the Christmas holidays. It was great to hear that faint Parisian accent once again. Eric said, "Pastor Jeff, I just want you to know that I will be baptized next week. I got it. I finally got it. I wanted to call and say thanks to you and all the people at The

Sanctuary. Tell them thanks. You were all so patient with me. I finally got it."

That was a particularly good Christmas.

Eric didn't know it, but he taught us some things about God and His sovereignty, and about the transforming power of God's truth. God didn't need us to reach Eric. We played our role. Others played theirs. God was in control of the whole process. We felt like failures for not producing a result that we had absolutely no power to produce.

I also learned about something about Kingdom Seekers that I would later describe as, *incipient sanctification*. The truth of God's Word has an affect on all people when that truth is honestly obeyed. Some Kingdom Seekers in their truthful struggle with sin and repentance, find that their lives are transformed into a healthier state. When these Kingdom Seekers give their lives to the King of Kings, they are much further down the road in the sanctification process. Eric's transformational mini-decisions of obedience to God's Word opened the door for increased health and vitality in the realm of his human relationships. His obedience to finally submit to the Lordship of Christ opened the door for an eternal relationship with the Father. Because so many other broken things in his life had already been repaired as he obeyed God's truth, he had fewer entanglements in his early walk with Christ.

Eric now leads the evangelism and outreach strategies of his new church.

Transformation is not the licensed property of the sacred space. Transformation is simply the natural Kingdom fruit of humble obedience to God's Word.

kingdom-expanders

4) INCARNATION

The Incarnation refers to the historic event when the eternal Agent of Creation, Jesus Christ, took on human flesh, walked as a man, and ultimately paid sin's price through his own sacrificial and atoning death and subsequent bodily resurrection. The Incarnation is history's centerpiece; it is a celestial event that will not be repeated. The saving work of Christ, and His subversive and counter-cultural instructions for Kingdom living brought about history's ultimate change.

In missiological writings, the term 'incarnational' can become a confusing term, often referring to two different ideas that are distinct from the traditional understanding of the word. The more common use of this word refers to Kingdom people 'moving in' and ministering among the needs of humanity. It speaks of bringing the "flesh" of the people of God to serve the Kingdom of God in the arena of brokenness. In this use of the term, the linkage is attached to the Christ-like actions of becoming a part of the brokenness in order to bring Good News. It is a missionary impulse in the best sense of the word.

The other, less common use of the term focuses the 'incarnation', not on the agent of Good News, but on its distressed recipient. This is a motivational source and power for change belonging to an altogether different realm. Kingdom leaders throughout history have found courage, patience, passion, compassion, and tireless persistence in the face of society's most thorny challenges all because they simply understood their mission of blessing in the most remarkable way. Look again at Matthew 25:

> *The King will reply, 'I tell you the truth, whatever you did for one of the least of these brothers of mine, you did for me.'* (Matthew 25:40)

The personal journals and the testimonies of many unsung heroes of the Kingdom record a unique way of seeing the prize of their ministry and service; some look at the wounded they are ministering to as their precious Savior, Jesus, Himself. To them, Jesus' words of, "whatever you did for one of the least of these brothers of mine, you did for me", was never intended to be warm and unfulfilled sentimentalism, but instead, a motivational mandate of the highest order. The question of 'worthy' or 'unworthy' candidates for the blessing of selfless Kingdom love becomes a ridiculous thought when they look at the wounded. Their care is reserved for Jesus. This elevates the focus of incarnational ministry to the highest of all places. It becomes a sacred act of worship reminiscent of a woman and an alabaster vial.

Ministry freely given to others as if being given to Jesus, Himself, is a powerful agent of change in two different and opposite directions. If you have ever been in a place of brokenness or need, and have been blessed enough to have unexpectedly received the selfless ministry of a brother or sister in Christ, you know the impact it has on the deep places of your soul. That love gift reached you in a way that you likely didn't conceive as possible. That touch brought back feeling to numb emotions. That unexpected measure of care gave you insight that even in your deep brokenness, you were of great value. You look back at those painful moments and see that in the midst of them you have experienced the love of Christ in a more profound way than any other season in life. Someone ministered to you with the unmeasured love that could only be given as an act of worship reserved exclusively for a Savior.

Radical unmerited love poured generously over the broken and rejected is the planet's most irresistible change agent. The doors of the Good News are pulled open wide.

The second direction that this kind of incarnational ministry has a potent change effect is upon the Kingdom servant himself. To anyone who has ministered in more than a casual, intermittent way, the reality of fatigue and burnout is ever present. There is no end to need. There is an unrelenting line of casualties, victims, and wounded wanting your attention. Fortunately for the professionals, we have been trained on how to handle this as mavens: maintain boundaries, work on our turf, and above all, keep a professional distance. Our rules help manage the chaos and keep us sane. Where would we be without the rules!

But the thought comes to most Kingdom leaders who surrendered to Kingdom ministry before ever knowing the professional rules, "I am now well-insulated, but am I effective? Where is the joy and passion that I once had in my service? Where is the transformation? Could I see Jesus living by these rules?' And we begin to question the axioms that were drilled into our heads in trade school. We begin to believe that we would gladly exchange the new professionalism for the old passion.

What can protect us from the fatigue of unyielding need without reducing us to ineffective professionalism? Changing our orientation on Whom we are serving.

Matthew 25 inspires us with the fact that we are not serving Jesus in some metaphorical way that could include any number of sacred activities. When it comes to the weak, the poor, and the marginalized, the ministry we offer is actually ministry to the person of Jesus Christ. It is a supreme act of worship and devotion. It arouses me as a worshipper to love recklessly without any professional confines.

Everything changes.

CHAPTER 9

THE MATRIX OF COMMUNITY

KINGDOM SOURCE	
DOMINION OF DARKNESS	**KINGDOM OF GOD**
BRAND EXPANDERS	KINGDOM EXPANDERS
group isolation	*interdependence*
SELF-SEEKERS	KINGDOM SEEKERS
isolation	*support*

FORM · SACRED COMMUNITY · SECULAR COMMUNITY · KINGDOM PRINCIPLE

One of the greatest blessings from heaven given to us on earth is the comfort and pleasure of knowing and being known. The contentment found in being accepted and the pre-packaged joy that comes with accepting others is the very foundation that authentic Christian community is built upon.

In Acts 2:44-47, we see a vivid picture of the transformative affect that true Kingdom community can have on the landscape it occupies. As the people of God were busy engaging in honest relationships with one another, a religious and very lonely world looked at their community with an envious eye. Their longings turned into curiosity, which in turn morphed into tiptoeing around the fringes until, being utterly convinced of their authenticity, they jumped unreservedly into their community . . . "And the Lord added to their number day by day those who were being saved." vs. 47 (ESV)

Unfortunately, honest community is not what we are conditioned to anticipate.

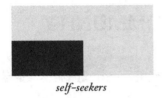

self-seekers

1) ISOLATION AND INDEPENDENCE

When someone breaks the law with a severe enough infraction, our society punishes him or her by isolating the convicted in a restricted environment away from the normalcy of his or her community. If the convicted persists in his aberrant patterns of behavior, he is further penalized through prohibiting his social interactions through the instrument of solitary confinement.

It would seem that short of the varying and complex ways to administer the death penalty, the cruelest punishment our society can engineer is the sentence of isolation. How ironic it is that isolation also happens to be the lifestyle of choice for the self-seeker. To this person, a self-inflicted prison of voluntary exclusion is more preferable than the humility of deconstructing a carefully crafted and meticulously refined image. The image projected is a mask to hide the reality of brokenness and personal defeat. The heroic measures taken to carefully hide feelings of personal inadequacy become an all too normal way of life for many.

Facing the ugly picture of intimate brokenness, the self-seeker has no place to turn for aid or solace. He has excluded himself from the help of a deity, and he has insulated himself from the benefit of community. He stands alone and accountable, and very much personifies the pitiable picture that William Henley paints in *Invictis*:

> *Beyond this place of wrath and tears Looms but the Horror of the shade, And yet the menace of the years Finds, and shall find, me unafraid. It matters not how strait the gate, How charged with punishments the scroll. I am the master of my fate: I am the captain of my soul.*

Unfortunately, his delicately self-fashioned image cannot afford the unsteadying luxury of community.

And so, as master and captain, the self-seeker stubbornly limps through the bloody carnage of a lifetime of broken relationships, never for a moment yielding to the nagging notion of personal responsibility.

Unfortunately, his delicately self-fashioned image cannot afford the unsteadying luxury of community.

brand-expanders

2) GROUP ISOLATION AND INDEPENDENCE

As we have already observed, the Kingdom of God flourishes when generous helpings of light are dished out in great big dollops and are lavishly applied to every area of life. In God's gracious plan, he made provision for the administration of this life-giving light through the church. As the Holy Spirit reveals opportunities for spiritual growth, revelations are made known and accountable, and together brothers and sisters are able to journey on the disciple's path.

But what happens to our sacred community when our only point of 'togetherness' is that of a corporate gathering? Where is the light of sacred accountability when my spiritual exchanges are reduced to the perfunctory greetings necessary for a well-timed crescendo at high noon? Who knows me well enough to care for me well?

When spiritual community is deprived of the life-giving oxygen of self-disclosure, darkness has found a sacred home. The dominion of darkness never inspires the honesty of personal admission, or the accountability that follows spiritual introspection. Darkness' strategy has always been very simple—let all the strugglers struggle alone. The dark reign doesn't seem to be offended by our congregating, passive listening, and melodic chanting—what is not permitted is our humble self-revelation.

Darkness inspires, sponsors, and promotes sacred isolation. In our independent solitude there is little chance of gaining ground in the disciples' task of resembling King Jesus. Pop culture's axiom of, "fake it 'til you make it," might be helpful in stumbling our way to higher proficiency in some outward pursuit, but has nothing to offer the would-be-disciple in his spiritual transformation. Pretense and darkness are kissing cousins.

In the same way that the self-seeker makes his way through a workday without any admission of weakness, side steps any conversation that might reveal a vulnerability, arrives home and punches the garage door opener only to disappear into the catacombs of his suburbia without any exchange that could be considered human interaction—so, the Brand-Expander designs his church attentively for the fragile needs of sacred self-seeker.

Entertain, inspire, and instruct—but never put the customer in a situation that could be uncomfortable.

Before I am too misunderstood, allow me to freely confess that I believe that the 'seeker-sensitive' movement has served the church well in many, many ways. The movement helped us understand the emotional, intellectual and spiritual barriers that stand in the way from a religiously uninitiated person's perspective. Before Rick Warren, Bill Hybels and a handful of others brought this idea to the forefront, countless churches blindly carried out weekly rituals without any thought to how foreign and strange their vernacular and customs were to the irreligious they were commissioned to reach. However, countless church planters and pastors have thoughtlessly tried to reproduce the novelty of the seeker assembly, with little consideration given to the transformative charge of the church. Essential to the disciples' transformation process is authentic, honest, and intimate community. Observe James' advice:

"Therefore, confess your sins to one another and pray for one another, that you may be healed. The prayer of a righteous person has great power as it is working." (James 5:15; ESV)

The days following the seeker movement ushered several alternate iterations of sacred assembly culminating in a gospel-centric pendulum swing that emphasizes the supremacy of the expository message. Again, another healthy correction to the preaching which had degenerated in many pulpits to become a diet of 'how to' self-help seminars scantily dressed in a spiritual miniskirt. The brand may have expanded, but the club member had not changed. A corrective shift was needed.

Yet even in our counteractive measures, we seem to have missed the point of Kingdom community. A well-articulated gospel-centric expository message delivering sacred community can still be a wonderful place to hide from the transformational power of humble self-confession. As we already observed, ortho-doxy without orthopraxy will soon become a lifeless superiority with little spiritual punch.

As long as our expectations of the disciple do not include the humility of authentic community and only requires weekly exer-cises in group-isolation, we have created adequate elbowroom for darkness to maneuver unhindered.

Kingdom transformation is unlikely.

kingdom-seekers

3) SUPPORT

Darkness thrives in murky conditions of isolation, separation and nondisclosure. In this habitat of self-seclusion, there is little opportunity for any hope, courage or optimism to take root be-cause seclusion fosters a more potent and overwhelming haze of discouragement. Emotionally and spiritually alone, we endure the empty journey, side by side, toward the land of dreariness and despair. The prince of darkness rubs his bony hands in gleeful triumph when secular and sacred alike prefer the pride of image to the humility of truth. The dark prince understands that man-kind, without aid of honest community, is on a one-way journey to desperate misery.

But darkness is not the only source of spiritual inspiration. Some, even in secular environments, have learned that transpar-ency and disclosure lead to healing and support. Where some have unsuccessfully searched for help in sacred communities, they found their help in the world outside the stained glass. They found a community of support.

In a support group, participants voluntarily provide one another with various types of help for a particular shared, usually burdensome, common struggle. The help may take the form of providing and evaluating relevant information, listening to and accepting others' experiences, and providing sympathetic understanding in efforts to establish a supportive shared environment for growth. The common themes in support groups are: telling the truth of one's journey, accepting one another, and offering aid and assistance to one another. Kingdom themes.

Truth, acceptance and mutual assistance, even in secular form, sound remarkably similar to ideas that we understand to originate from Light, and are to serve as blueprints for sacred communities of faith. What the Kingdom-seeker instinctively yearns and urgently searches for is truthful and authentic support.

The Kingdom-seeker in the honesty of his quest is so very close to the Kingdom. With the light found in humility, he becomes open to outside sources of help. With the truth of self-disclosure he more accurately evaluates his present condition. What joy and deliverance would this Kingdom-seeker experience if a sacred struggler would share with him the Source of two more powerful assets to be found in his transformation: an indwelling Spirit to empower change, and an unchanging Book of Truth to guide the way.

With the lessons learned in secular communities of support coupled with a spiritually empowered and directed life—this Kingdom-seeker turned Kingdom Expander becomes one of King Jesus' mightiest men of valor.

In community, darkness has no chance.

kingdom-expanders

4) INTERDEPENDENCE

The western world's fascination with
independence seems to be a strange blip
on the historical experience of community.
Autonomy might be a celebrated pursuit
in many evangelical traditions, but seems
peculiarly vacant from the interdependent
relationships that we see in the example of
the early church.

The western world's fascination with independence seems to be a strange blip on the historical experience of community. Autonomy might be a celebrated pursuit in many evangelical traditions, but seems peculiarly vacant from the interdependent relationships that we see in the example of the early church.

The New Testament uses a term to describe the relational interdependence of Christ's body, *koinonia*. The common, albeit inadequate translation is, 'fellowship.' This is not the most helpful translation because it carries with it a modern connotation of a loose gathering of friends. *Koinonia* is a much more deliberate concept conveying the idea of a community holding things in common. The first Christ-followers had a *koinonia* that is well described as an interdependent community; they were a fellowship that shared.

The first sharing among the first church was sharing in the Holy Spirit. Paul refers to the "*koinonia* of the Holy Spirit" or the "community of the Holy Spirit" (2 Corinthians 13:14). This Spirit was the very foundation of the Christians' community, or common life. Out of that common Spirit, the early Christians shared much more; they had their whole lives in common (again see, Acts 2:42-47; 4:32-37). Having everything in common meant that no one claimed ownership of their possessions. Ownership was a master's privilege and the first believers clearly understood the nature of their relationship with the King. Everything was at the disposal of the community for the common good.

It was a community that shared in the joys and the sacrifices of following Jesus.

One of the values of the church-planting network that we were starting in Toronto was the priority of giving God our 'first fruit'. We believed that if we were to ask our people to tithe, that we as a family of faith should lead by example. Our commitment was ten-percent to our denomination's mission funding strategy called the Cooperative Program. We felt that this helped enable our church to resource Kingdom work in places around the world that our network would never personally touch. Additionally, a large portion of our budget went to help support the local church plants that we were starting across the region.

We developed a spending priority schedule. Priority number one: giving to world missions. Priority number two: giving to our church plants. Priority number three: funding the home-front. We felt that articulating these priorities upfront would help direct our faith against the temptations found in the inevitable seasons of lack.

God clearly honored this faith step numerous times as we stretched ourselves to try to reach the next community, but never more clearly than during the summer of 2009.

I was no longer in my role as pastor of The Sanctuary, but was often invited to attend staff meetings when I was in town. The report on this particular meeting was that it was apparent that the summer was rough on local giving. Money was short. Brad Klinck, our executive pastor said, "We have enough cash to pay this month's salaries or this month's missions giving—but not both. What should we do?"

Pastor Peter Roebbelen skillfully took the reigns of leadership. He said, "Well guys, what will do?" And then sat in silence. One by one each staff member said, "We have got to put God first in this." It seemed unanimous.

Then Peter posed a second question, "Guys, I'm a little more established in life than most of you. If you do not get this paycheck, will you be able to pay your rent?" Each offered their response. The answer was "no" for all. Peter replied, "In light of this reality, what should we do?" The staff quietly and yet in unison said, "We must honor God in this. This is a time where our trust in God is being tested."

I sat there humbled as I listened to the faith of these men and women of God. They began to pray together. It was not a tearful prayer of self-pity. It was a unified declaration of faith. This staff believed that God had called them to this assignment and that somehow God would provide for their needs.

The next Sunday, smack in the middle of the dog days of August, the nets began to break with God's provision. It was the single biggest offering in our history. The people of God wanted the joy of sharing in the suffering of their leaders—and so they gave sacrificially.

Koinonia experienced.

Individualism is much too self-centered of an
aspiration to be fanned by a Kingdom Source.

Implicit to the theology of a common Spirit amongst Christ-followers is an equally common synergy and collaboration. As uncommon as this experience may be in Western Christianity, it is not without ample witness throughout history and around our globe. Whenever you see a great movement of God spread through a geography, you will always see the Spirit's hallmarks of individual and corporate collaboration. Individualism is much too self-centered of an aspiration to be fanned by a Kingdom Source.

Critical to the implications of biblical community is the humility to lay down our hard-won independence and learn a much better way—a way of transparence and trust. Interdependence does not mean becoming pathetic and less capable of moving forward and taking new ground. In fact it is just the opposite. We choose the humility of interdependence in order to become stronger — to do even greater things than ever could be accomplished in isolation.

Independence's weakness is the pride of self-sufficiency—whether it is individual or corporate. Interdependence's strength is the humility of acknowledged weakness, individual or corporate, that allows the strength of God to fortify limitations. Sometimes God may do this through a Divine touch. Most often His strengthening work is performed through the blessing of His interdependent community.

Recalling the days of my childhood, I remember glimpses of how Jack Conner and Henry Blackaby led a couple of very small churches to accomplish something astonishing. Both leaders highly valued Paul's metaphor of the body and spoke of it often. They led their two congregations to understand and experience interdependence and the spiritual punch that it delivers to everyone connected in that local body. But as uncommon as this is to many people's experience, it is still more understood than the next level of Kingdom interdependence—corporate collaboration.

As often as these two pastors spoke on the theme of the Body, they spoke about the Kingdom of God. They understood that as pastors, they had a divine accountability to lead their churches to become spiritually healthy. However, their spiritual maturity informed them that spiritual health and an aggressive Kingdom agenda cannot be separated. To Jack and Henry, corporate health was not the goal, it was the means to the goal. The goal was always expanding the Kingdom of God. Not only was it the means to the goal, but it was also the method to the means. The result of focusing a church inward is a congregation of flabby spiritual consumers. The necessity of developing leaders to serve the consumers is a somewhat positive byproduct, but it cannot compare to the kind of leadership that is developed when a church cultivates and deploys its leaders on a Kingdom agenda that is outside of its insulating walls. In Kingdom-expanding fashion, Jack and Henry pointed the churches under their stewardship outward.

Kingdom interdependence dictates that corporate collaboration becomes normal.

Kingdom interdependence dictates that corporate collaboration becomes normal. When the assignment is greater than resources at hand (and it always is), interdependence moves from an option to a necessity. As these two Kingdom leaders surveyed the geography that surrounded them, they found numerous cities, towns and villages that needed a positive expression of Christ in their midst. New churches must be planted. And so these two churches teamed up to plant new congregations throughout the area. There was a constant demand for new leaders, so they were developed in the churches and sent out. There was an interdependent synergy between the congregations that felt like family. It was a beautiful expression of a selfless Kingdom culture.

Today, we see outcroppings of this corporate interdependence showing up all over North America. Kingdom-hearted church planters are shifting from 'planting a church' in a community, to 'churching a community.' They have grown past the idea of success being defined by the number of people on the benches. They honestly believe a quaint little notion that success is measured in the number of people in heaven. And so they are setting up strategies that will be able to evangelize the greatest amount of people in their region. Church planting networks are being developed that share resources, personnel and even finances in order to interdependently leverage varied strengths for a much greater Kingdom impact.

God's plan for His Kingdom is not individualistic autonomy. Isolation is inspired from a far darker realm. It is the genius of the Body working interdependently that propels unstoppably the great purposes of the Kingdom.

God's plan for His Kingdom is not individualistic autonomy. Isolation is inspired from a far darker realm. It is the genius of the Body working interdependently that propels unstoppably the great purposes of the Kingdom.

Collectively and synergistically synced under one King's instructions, hell's gates cannot stand.

CHAPTER 10

THE MATRIX OF LOVE

KINGDOM SOURCE		
	DOMINION OF DARKNESS	KINGDOM OF GOD
SACRED LOVE	BRAND EXPANDERS *storage*	KINGDOM EXPANDERS *agape*
SECULAR LOVE	SELF-SEEKERS *eros*	KINGDOM SEEKERS *phileo*
FORM		
	KINGDOM PRINCIPLE	

Our experience with love, both how we express it and how we receive it, is tied inescapably to where we get our sense of self. As we travel through the matrix, we will ask ourselves one simple question: Does our sense of identity come from ourselves *(eros)?* From family ties and people who are more like us *(storge)?* From whom we enjoy associating with *(phileo)?* Or, from God, Himself *(agape)?*

The answer to that question may reveal much as to my quadrant condition.

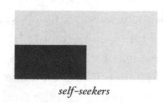

self-seekers

1) EROS (ἔρως)

The Greek language provides us with four words for love: *Eros, Storge, Phileo,* and *Agape.* One can easily recognize the word *"eros"* as the root of the word "erotic." But it has a little more to it than merely sexual desire. This is a love that seeks to satisfy an appetite, whether for sex, food, affirmation, or comfort.

In a lot of ways, this type of love defines the worst of western culture and sadly a percentage of Western Christianity.

My friend Mark has an awareness of God that fluctuates among Gnosticism, fearful reverence and anger depending on the current circumstances of life. His flirtations with "Christianity" are generated by his needs of self-preservation or pain avoidance— depending on the severity of his latest misstep. Consequently, his relationships with others are very similar. At the first sign of rejection or disagreement or pain, he hoists his defenses and closes people out. He equates love with the agreement of his views and the fulfillment of his desires. Mark's long-term relationships have been reduced to an ever-shrinking list of compliant personalities who acquiesce to the rules of his overgrown ego.

Mark is mostly alone.

We all experience glimpses of this *eros*-love and wouldn't be whole without it. But this is the depth of love that a self-seeker chooses to survive in. The shallow existence lived in *eros*-love seeks by all means possible to find fulfillment by satiating appetites of the moment. In a lot of ways, this type of love defines the worst of western culture and sadly a percentage of Western Christianity. In this polluted mode of understanding, God's blessings equal a fulfillment of my every selfish desire. It is spiritually fatal to love's object because God's pleasure is only determined by the circumstances experienced. God becomes as capricious as my circumstances and He's soon ditched for a more direct line to self-satisfaction.

A life lived in the shallow waters of *eros*-love
will inevitably leave a self-seeker alone
and unloved.

A life lived in the shallow waters of *eros*-love will inevitably leave a self-seeker alone and unloved.

brand-expanders

2) STORGE (στοργή)

James went to Christian High School and Christian college, got a job as a consultant with a reputable firm and lived in the suburbs where he sent his kids to Christian schools and thus continued the tradition. In the early years of his young family, James and his wife took their kids to a fashionable new church that had just the right balance of edgy music and solid biblical teaching. Their kids were happy, James and his wife were happy. Things were perfect.

Their church did a series on evangelism that was very inspiring and a little convicting. James had to do something. He went out and dropped flyers in their neighbors' mailboxes that explained their church programs and creatively enticed them to attend. James prayed hard that some of his unsaved neighbors would check out the programs the church had created for the community.

One family, two doors down, responded to the invitation and came to the worship service. James was so pumped. They attended faithfully for a few months, but then, for some mysterious reason, they stopped attending altogether. Rather than ask what was going on, James repeated an already known-to-be effective strategy: he began placing flyers in their mailbox for upcoming church conferences where they could once again be inspired by well-known speakers and a free lunch.

Months passed before James saw his neighbors again. The next time they met, the husband was packing to leave. Infidelity had shown its ugly head and the couple was going their separate ways. "I'm so sorry to hear that," said James. Without skipping a beat he offered, "You know, we have a popular divorce recovery class at church . . ."

A characteristic of being human is an attraction to the things that most affirm who we are. This characteristic is rooted in an exclusive love for the things that look, act, and resemble who we are and validate our delicate sensibilities. *Storge* could best be described as a sort of self-affirming nationalism, whether ethnic, political, familial, or socio-economical. *Storge*-love is a love that is reserved for the people who are most like us.

It's our family thing.

Donald McGavran, who first popularized the notion of the *homogenous* principle in his book, *Understanding Church Growth*, described the advantages of those who become Christians without crossing racial, linguistic or class barriers. He maintained that the barriers to the acceptance of the Gospel are more often more sociological than they are theological. The hypothesis behind it is that people tend to reject the gospel not because they think it is false, but because it strikes them as foreign and alien. They envision that in order to become Christ-followers that they must renounce their own culture, lose their own identity, and most heinous of all, betray their own people. Taking some themes from the book of Galatians, McGavran's answer was to create communities of faith that construct the fewest cultural barriers to a specific people group so that the Gospel could be heard without extraneous interference.

Without debating the merits or shortcomings implicit in McGavran's theory, a casual observation of Western Christianity demonstrates clearly that he has had a massive impact on the way we do church. Variations of his thinking became the standard operating system of the church growth movement. Beginning in the mid 1980's, pastors of every stripe have been busy identifying and describing their target group and tweaking their communication strategies to try to reach it. For many, it was a healthy exercise of putting legs to Paul's personal testimony:

> *To the weak I became weak, that I might win the weak. I have become all things to all people, that by all means I might save some. I do it all for the sake of the gospel.* (1 Corinthians 9:22-23 ESV)

However, not all are so purely motivated. The applications derived from the homogeneous principle can be equally applied to the selfish desires of the Brand-Expander. Instead of a missionary's selfless love of adapting methods and models to the cultural needs of the lost, some have established their own preferential methods and models and require the lost to fit in. If they don't fit, do we really need them?

In this space, the good intentions of the homogenous principle become hijacked for a much less demanding version. *Homocentricity*, that is, having the same center, became the pursuit of the well-oiled brand-expanding church. We want to associate with people who have preferences most like ours. And so, our target audience becomes easily identified and described. It is us.

Our communication strategies are not complicated either—what do we want to hear? Our mediums for transmitting the message can be easily focused as well—sacred radio, sacred television, sacred print sources—whatever the budget allows.

We plug in our nickels, fire up the machinery
and watch our return on investment
start rolling in.

We plug in our nickels, fire up the machinery and watch our return on investment start rolling in.

Nice congregations filled with nice people, that coincidentally enough, fit in perfectly with the systems we have designed. Church can be a really nice place if you know what you're doing. Of course not everyone will fit in. But, you can't please everyone . . .

After all, there are other churches that deal with the broken people.

kingdom-seekers

3) PHILEO (φιλία)

This love term is a little more common in everyday vernacular; we know that it means 'brotherly love.' This is the kind of love that allows for close friendships, for family-like relationships apart from family ties, for a community of people who have an honest desire to do good for each other. *Phileo*-love describes earnestness for the welfare of others.

It is familiar territory for Kingdom Seekers.

As I was writing this book, I skipped over this section several times. It is the one white space in my manuscript. I wasn't satisfied with any picture that I was painting to describe this activity. Three times before I had written word pictures of this *phileo*-love, and each time I had sensed that what I had written was not, 'it.'

Highlight and delete. Start over.

My publisher's deadline is now on Monday. It is the weekend and I still have a big *phileo*-love blank.

But this book is not the only thing going on in my world. Two months ago, my father, who is seventy-five, was diagnosed with liver and pancreas cancer—it is a terminal verdict. This news devastated our family—my dad who was so full of life began to quickly wither almost before our eyes. My weeks are full of airplanes and hotels, and my weekends were committed to a new and urgent priority of spending every possible moment with my dad. This curse of cancer came with an unexpected blessing of some of the most intimate moments with the man I have loved the longest and most. We reminisced together of a lifetime of God's faithfulness and the Kingdom legacy of generations that now follow him because of the grace he received in 1967. God has been so good.

This weekend, as I prepare to wrap the book up, we had to commit my dad to palliative care in hospice. His pain is overcoming him, his strength is almost gone, and he is so ready to be with King Jesus. Two weeks ago, yellow from being jaundiced, he joked that being in his 'golden years' was not quite what he expected. That twinkle in his eye is now a faint flicker. He lies in his bed barely resembling the man he was only a few weeks ago. His once strong tradesman arms, now tiny, still display the colorful evangelism bracelet he wears to declare his allegiance to Jesus. We love him so much and are very, very sad.

I already miss him.

I and so many others. You would expect family members to mourn. And we are. Hopefully members of one's faith community as well. And they are.

He became acquainted with my dad and was forced to rethink some of his long-held biases. In becoming open to the messenger, he started to become open to the Message.

But what about George?

George has been my dad's neighbor for the past two years. He is about ten years my dad's junior and the two became friends almost as soon as my mom and dad moved into his neighborhood. If you were going to describe George, you'd probably say, "George is just a really great guy." He really is. He is not yet a Christ-follower, though my dad has shared the Gospel with him on numerous occasions—but he is a man who understands *phileo*-love.

George is a busy guy. His aged parents live in his home and he cares for them. His daughter, a single mom, drops her children off at 'grandpa's'—and he cares for them. In between these responsibilities, and his work—he somehow finds the energy to notice others around him. He mows my parent's lawn, shovels their snow, checks in to fix anything he can find. Over and over he would say to my mom, "Any time, day, night, midnight, whatever—if you need help with Allan, please call me. That's what neighbors do." George is a really great guy.

George, the neighbor, is mourning too.

George is a Kingdom-seeker. Not too long ago you would characterize him as a man who was closed to the message of the Gospel—he was simply not interested. He became acquainted with my dad and was forced to rethink some of his long-held biases. In becoming open to the messenger, he started to become open to the Message. Even though I speak of George in his current 'pre-Christian' state, he is a man who shares a selfless love that is Kingdom inspired. His unselfish care for my parents is an impulse motivated from no other spiritual realm other than heaven. It is altruism devotedly directed toward a fellow neighbor as a gift of *phileo*-love. He is not yet a follower of the King, yet his *phileo*-love seems almost 'Christian.'

The resemblance in love is seen by the Kingdom source that has inspired it. It is selfless and directed outward apart from any expectations of benefits derived. *Phileo*-love exists to bless.

By the time anyone will read these words, my dad will have spent many unimaginably wonderful days at the feet of the One whom he loved so well for many years. Perhaps, one final legacy of my dad's faith will be that George will complete his heart's quest and come to know the One who inspired his generous *phileo*-love.

kingdom-expanders

4) AGAPE (ἀγάπη)

When Christ mended the ear that Peter had severed, knowing the soldier he healed would be His captor, He was expressing *agape*-love.

When Christ mended the ear that Peter had severed, knowing the soldier he healed would be His captor, He was expressing *agape*-love. It is a lavish and self-sacrificing love that is generously dished out without thought of merit or virtue. It is the love that God has for all people that is expressed so beautifully in John 3:16.

For true *agape*-love to exist, it assumes a benefactor of limitless emotional resources. It presupposes that the love-giver has no need to receive in order to persistently give. It speaks of one so inexhaustible that he lacks nothing in himself and never could be in want. It is an impossible love for frail, needy human creatures.

Unless they know Someone.

Let me introduce you to a Christ-follower whose life has impacted many in my circle of influence. We will call him 'Sam.'

His story begins in the darkest days of Cambodia's killing fields where Pol Pot's rampage snuffed out 1.7 million of his countrymen's lives.

The boy who crawled out of the grave, and the man he became . . .

After two years of near starvation and forced labor at the hands of the Khmer Rouge, Sam's eleven siblings and his parents were forcibly taken by soldiers and dragged to the edge of an open grave. "Today, we will destroy you," the soldiers yelled. And they did exactly that. To save bullets, his family members were simply hacked and beaten with clubs and axes. One by one they were piled on top of each other in a horrific entanglement of dead neighbors and family members. The scene was repeated throughout the country.

On this day, a small miracle took place. Thirteen year-old Sam, grazed and stunned, watched the killers in silence as he lay on his dead father's body in the mass grave. At nightfall, when it appeared to be safe, Sam, the lone survivor, struggled to pull himself out from underneath the heavy corpses of his family and to escape with his life.

Left alone, afraid and deeply emotionally scarred, Sam was now faced with a life sentence of understandable bitterness and anger. "Depression pursued me like a shadow," says Sam. "Hope-lessness was the greatest enemy of my life. Why had I survived?"

Despite the horrors of his childhood, Sam now is able to look back and see the hand of God on his life. He was able to immigrate to Toronto as a refugee, and to begin the challenge of building a new life in a strange land. Through various circumstances and the generous love of faithful Christ-followers, Sam trusted his future with Jesus as his Lord and Savior.

Trusting Christ with his past was the journey yet to come.

In personally experiencing Christ's forgiveness, Sam was now forced to reconcile Jesus' command on him to forgive his enemies—specifically, his family's executioners. This inhuman requirement set Sam on a pursuit for the true meaning of forgiveness. Struggling with this Kingdom condition launched Sam out on a life-long journey of studying and obeying the Scriptures. He was a man after God's own heart.

As Sam grew in the understanding of his salvation's price, he was unable to shake the inevitable question of his own willingness to forgive. This led him to the much more difficult journey of forgiving his family's killers—in person.

Sam took the long and painful journey back to his village. After some research he located and presented his family's executioners with gifts of scarves and Bibles as a symbol of his own forgiveness of them. The first soldier that he approached seemed unmoved. He said nothing and offered nothing. The second soldier he located broke down and asked for forgiveness in kind.

These men, who continue to live under this repressive regime themselves, could not understand his motive. Who could? This kind of forgiveness is not of this world.

Sam soon returned and with his own life's savings, started a school for the village's children. Five students in the first class that he educated were children of the unrepentant executioner. Sam loved them too.

After years of suffering, Sam was finally at peace.

Today, Sam is proclaiming the freedom
of forgiveness in Christ through planting
churches in the former killing fields
of his family.

But God would require even more of him. Sam permanently left the freedom and safety of Toronto to move back to his Cambodian hometown where, for three years, he taught courageous young pastors at a Bible college.

Today, Sam is proclaiming the freedom of forgiveness in Christ through planting churches in the former killing fields of his family.

The testimony of Sam's life vividly demonstrates the otherworldly power of *agape*-love. Mere mortals have no capacity to live on this plane. But a Christ-follower's humble submission to the King opens wide the channels through which His nature can flow.

Christ's *agape*-love lived out through faithful believers always conveys a Kingdom-expanding affect. Darkness cannot comprehend it.

CHAPTER 11

THE MATRIX OF AUTHORITY

KINGDOM SOURCE	
DOMINION OF DARKNESS	**KINGDOM OF GOD**
BRAND EXPANDERS	KINGDOM EXPANDERS
corporate identity	*the King*
SELF-SEEKERS	KINGDOM SEEKERS
me	*God, as I understand Him*

FORM

SACRED AUTHORITY

SECULAR AUTHORITY

KINGDOM PRINCIPLE

To this point, we have looked at four distinct Kingdom values, each expressed from a very different quadrant of the matrix: *energy* (how we are motivated), *community* (how we relate), *change* (how we grow), and *love* (how we bless). In each of these four Kingdom themes, we could easily observe radically different approaches to the same concept. Each quadrant was profoundly influenced by the spiritual source that had inspired its pattern of behavior while secondarily influenced by sacred/secular forms in which they exist. Finally, we will examine how each quadrant selects its *authority* for its definitive accountability.

Implicit to a healthy concept of the Kingdom of God is a clear understanding of God's sovereign authority over time, matter, and space—specifically, our time, our matter, and our space.

In whatever way that we choose to espouse this authority, our attitudes and actions find their natural transcendent expression.

self-seekers

1) ME

Eden's catastrophic fall was a consequence of Divine authority usurped. The first man's and woman's death-decision was motivated by darkness' appeal to some kind of celestial equality. The fruit of this line of thinking was, and always is, hubris. Inspired by the dominion of darkness, Adam and Eve lost contact with reality and began to nurture an overestimation of their own personhood and capabilities. By succumbing to the temptation of becoming equal to their Creator (One whom they knew intimately), should demonstrate with precision that hubris has no bounds or limits. Adam's and Eve's desire for godhood led to masterminding a spiritual coup that would replace their accountability to their Author with a free state of personal inclinations. They would be their own authority. They would be like God.

And they were ruined.

Flip through the calendar of history and it is clear to see that nothing has changed; darkness' charm to the self-seeker has always been the self-becoming of his or her own god. The standard for this decision-making is a constantly moving target that looks to the vacillating mores of society, or worse, the fickle moods of my imperfect personality. Right and wrong, fully reduced to becoming phantoms of a bygone era, conveniently change on demand to accommodate my circumstances.

Authority does have its privileges.

But it is not all fun and games. With great authority also comes great responsibility. Sitting uncomfortably alone and unaided on the throne seat of judgment, the self-seeker is forced to render eternally binding rulings on matters that will serve as the foundation for his, and his family's future. As captain and master, the self-seeker has no higher authority to advise him. He sits unaccompanied and sifts through opinions and personal desires in order to make his best bet.

And the stakes are high.

Apart from a gracious touch of the King of Kings, the self-seeker is ruined.

The self-seeker's desperate situation is pitiable. He feels the whole weight of the consequences of his decisions, but has no authoritative resources, other than imperfect inclinations, on which to draw. He blithely dreams of his freedom until he awakens to find that his liberty has been a snare that has strongly tied the trajectory of his future to the brokenness of his past. He has no innate abilities to stop the train-wreck that his voracious appetite for power has set into motion. From the carnage witnessed in sullied and spoiled relationships, it is easy to see that unauthorized authority, in fact, has no authority at all.

Apart from a gracious touch of the King of Kings, the self-seeker is ruined.

brand-expanders

2) CORPORATE IDENTITY

In the same mutinous waters where self-seekers prefer to voyage, their religious relatives find an open opportunity to hoist their traitorous sails. Flying high the colors of their dark allegiance, the *SS Expander* boasts of past exploits and future conquests through the macabre scene of the floating entrails of one unsuspecting vessel after another. The spotless white sails and the knotless timbers were camouflage enough to convince other sailors of their friendly intentions. Not until the flash of the first mortar was spotted did the naïve seafarers realize that they were not of the same country. Though they looked so similar, their treacherous maneuvers demonstrated that their authority came from a different source.

A source as different as night is from day.

When King Jesus walked amongst us in the physical form, his prayer was overheard and penned so that subsequent generations of His followers could understand the nature of Kingdom citizenship. It appears that Kingdom citizens were to demonstrate the great glory of God by living together in selfless unity. Jesus prayed:

> *"I do not ask for these only, but also for those who will believe in me through their word, that they may all be one, just as you, Father, are in me, and I in you, that they also may be in us, so that the world may believe that you have sent me. The glory that you have given me I have given to them, that they may be one even as we are one, I in them and you in me, that they may become perfectly one, so that the world may know that you sent me and loved them even as you loved me."* (John 17:20-23 ESV)

It seemed to Jesus that effective evangelism was a spontaneous action resulting from God's glory being obvious amongst God's people. How would God's glory be seen? By Kingdom people acting in unity as one. In this Kingdom culture, the 'outsiders' would take notice and understand something of the King's love for His people. Perfect Kingdom oneness was Jesus' prayer.

Soon we would read of its answer:

> *Now the full number of those who believed were of one heart and soul, and no one said that any of the things that belonged to him was his own, but they had everything in common. And with great power the apostles were giving their testimony to the resurrection of the Lord Jesus, and great grace was upon them all.* (Acts 4:32-33 ESV)

Acts 4:32-33 parallels Acts 2:42-47 and documents both the oneness of the first church and the effects of that unity. This church was comprised of a loyal band of followers united under and obedient to the authority of King Jesus. Their love and devotion for their King was marked by their love and devotion for one another. Their willingness to sacrifice for their King was inextricably linked to their willingness to sacrifice for one another. The power of their testimony of was correlated to the power of their community. The authority of their community was wholly dependent on their submission to the authority of their King. God's glory was revealed through unity, with unity came God's authority, and with God's authority came credible evangelism.

The King's culture lived out by His selfless subjects became a compelling draw too wonderful to miss.

Spiritual authority underwritten by a singular devotion to Christ is a devastating weapon to the realm of darkness. Hell has no defense. The King's watermark is seen in the surprising harmony between Kingdom citizens. And so the Divine directive: first, allegiance to King; second, to countrymen, and; third, an outcome of unearthly authority.

The imprisoned Apostle Paul pleaded for his beloved Philippian friends to experience firsthand the unstoppable power of oneness in the life and death spiritual battle that they were engaging:

Only let your manner of life be worthy of the gospel of Christ, so that whether I come and see you or am absent, I may hear of you that you are standing firm in one spirit, with one mind striving side by side for the faith of the gospel and not frightened in anything by your opponents. This is a clear sign to them of their destruction, but of your salvation, and that from God. (Philippians 1:27-28 ESV)

Succinctly put: the Kingdom of God inspires unity under a King; darkness inspires uniformity under anyone or anything else.

Enter, the Brand-Expander.

When Christ is pulled off the top shelf of our sacred allegiance, what is put in His place? We can usually find any number of decent and devastating replacements to uniform our corporate identity. When we do, a competitive brand is created. It works tirelessly enticing us to compliantly line up in single file behind it. It can come in the form of a personality, a church, a network, a denomination, or a theological category. All forms have the potential for great good. None are evil in themselves. Evil arrives when the call to expansion motivated by competition and/or self-preservation replaces the call to die with Christ. In this exchange we get a pungent whiff of sulfur from a form we call sacred.

Truly, truly, I say to you, unless a grain of wheat falls into the earth and dies, it remains alone; but if it dies, it bears much fruit. Whoever loves his life loses it, and whoever hates his life in this world will keep it for eternal life. (John 12:24-25 ESV)

The Gospel writers recorded the corporate identity of our King's Kingdom as He delivered numerous metaphors of the nature of His Reign. It seems to have less to do corporate success than it does with corporate humility and self-sacrifice. Success is a managed devotion. Self-sacrifice is a trusting abandonment. Success gives glory to the successful. Self-sacrifice gives glory to the Resurrection. Success is a term of addition. Self-sacrifice is a term of exponential multiplication. Success is man's plan for life. Self-sacrifice is God's.

The source that inspires some sacred leadership to rally the troops around a corporate identity may not always originate from a holy place. Its spiritual source is revealed by the selfless sacrifice that it inspires toward following King Jesus.

For we are the aroma of Christ to God among those who are being saved and among those who are perishing. (2 Corinthians 2:15 ESV)

kingdom-seekers

3) "GOD, AS I UNDERSTAND HIM"

For the Kingdom-seeker, the whole issue of spiritual authority is a deeply troubling one. Although his formal instruction may have taught him that the idea of an Ultimate Authority is a crutch for the weak and a pleasing myth for the intellectually challenged, his spirit gets some different signals. He grasps at how to express this eternal longing and uses unconventional language that some of the initiated do not appreciate.

To many faithful churchgoers, any sentence that begins with, "Well, God, as I understand him . . ." sends cold shivers down the spine. As our blood pressure rises, we struggle to contain our real feelings: "How could some spiritual neophyte have the self-pretentious nerve to offer his own depraved understanding of God as some type of authoritative characterization? Look to the Book you heathen!"

But before we start bending over to pick up stones, let's try to walk a few steps in the sandals of a Kingdom-seeker.

There are many around us who are at a significant spiritual disadvantage. Growing up in our ever-increasing post-modern western world, there has been little exposure to the Good News of Jesus that has either been healthy or readily available. For many, the only observable examples of 'Jesus' people' are the socially stunted who so crave notoriety that they brashly pronounce unconstructive statements and opinions for the media to gobble up. The caricatures of the Gospel that many Kingdom Seekers witness seem dark and unconvincing. But this does not mean that he is left without light.

> *Since what may be known about God is plain to them, because God has made it plain to them. For since the creation of the world God's invisible qualities—his eternal power and divine nature—have been clearly seen, being understood from what has been made, so that people are without excuse.* (Romans 1:19-20 NIV)

Although we all stand accountable at the judgment seat of Christ, God in His grace reveals His light to the Kingdom-seeker through means such as creation and conscience.

> *For when Gentiles, who do not have the law, by nature do what the law requires, they are a law to themselves, even though they do not have the law. They show that the work of the law is written on their hearts, while their conscience also bears witness, and their conflicting thoughts accuse or even excuse them on that day when, according to my gospel, God judges the secrets of men by Christ Jesus.* (Romans 2:14-16 NIV)

In God's compassionate desire that none should perish (2 Peter 3:9), He communicates to the Kingdom-seeker in ways that he can understand. Through creation and conscience, this seeker is given opportunity to obey the Voice of Truth. "God," as this spiritual pilgrim "understands Him," begins to come into focus.

Though a narcissistic religious pitchman may cloud the view, God's omnipotent power and unyielding love can cut through it all with the whisper of His still small voice. His whisper is light. As the Kingdom-seeker responds faithfully to that light, more light is revealed. Light always leads to its Kingdom source—the Good News of salvation through the substitutionary death and resurrection of the King of Kings. Failure to respond to the Light aligns us with the same eternal fate as darkness. We are without excuse.

Unexpected Light

Let's go back to the Kingdom-seeker's clumsy way of expressing his spiritual reality. Without aid of a religious pedigree he makes personal observations of the spiritual climate that surrounds him. He witnesses a deep devotion from various peoples to the gods of their religion. He recognizes that they are involved in something that he doesn't understand—but somehow innately respects. He doesn't have a faith, yet somehow deeply craves it. Seeing the genuineness of the diverse passion for a wide range of religious expressions, he makes the only logical conclusion that he can with the information that he has: "If there is a God, all religious paths must lead to the same place."

This acknowledgement, as upsetting as it might be to those who take their religion seriously, is actually an accurate response. It paves the way for a Kingdom Expander to introduce the Light of the Gospel. The Kingdom-seeker has witnessed the devotion of diverse religious peoples. He has taken note of the sacrifice and spiritually focused effort directed toward numerous unknown deities. His rational supposition of "all religions must lead to the same place," is a giftwrapped opportunity for any Christ-follower who is looking for an opportunity to engage.

"I totally agree," might be a shocking answer to hear from the lips of someone this seeker thought was a little too religious. He didn't expect this. Were not evangelical Christians supposed to be superior to everybody else? Bewildered, he needs further clarification.

"So, you think that all religions are the same?" the seeker inquires. "Absolutely," the witness of Christ answers. He clarifies, "All religions travel in the very same direction: away from God. Including the Christian one."

A timid question is induced, "So you don't believe in the Christian religion?" "No, I don't. Religion is man's way to climb to God. All religions have some system to follow in order to gain favor with God. When Jesus walked the earth, there were plenty of religions—He didn't come to start one more. He came to do something that no religion could ever do. Repair the brokenness of man caused by sin."

The Kingdom-seeker, in responding honestly to the light given him, comes face to face with the best news that he could ever hear.

Unexpected light from a gracious King.

kingdom-expanders

4) THE KING OF KINGS

In the very breath before Jesus articulated his Kingdom assignment for those who would be His subjects, He qualified the scope of His authority,

> *All authority in heaven and on earth has been given to me. Go therefore* . . . (Matthew 28:18-19 ESV)

It seemed from the perspective of the One who whispered the universe into existence, that it was not too troubling of a task to supply His subjects with what they needed to accomplish His bidding. Scripture teaches us that with the commissioning of His disciple for Kingly pursuits comes prepackaged the Kingly authority to prepare the way. It all seems so simple and obvious. The King of Kings supplies His humble subjects with all that is needed to accomplish His will.

It is simple and obvious and yet it is anthrax to our pride. With a Divine assignment and a Heavenly authority to accomplish it, there is little opportunity to fan the ever-glowing embers of human pride.

One would think . . .

But what happens when the King's instructions are ill conceived? What if He calls us to something absurd? What if He leads us to something that is far too reminiscent of pouring water on an altar and calling down heavenly fire? Are modern day subjects to be obedient to the tackle the ludicrous?

Allow me to share a story . . .

Saddam, Salaam, and the Well-timed Psalm

On March 19, 2003, the world was angry, proud, afraid, excited and confused when George W. Bush and Tony Blair declared war, once again, on Iraq. This second round of hostilities was named "Operation: Shock and Awe" after a military strategy centered on the *Doctrine of Rapid Dominance* was designed to eradicate Iraq's possession of weapons of mass destruction, and swap a malevolent dictatorship for western style democracy. The deadly fireworks and plumes of smoke and debris were beamed into the world's family rooms, in real time, almost as a surreal edition of *24* starring Jack Bauer.

In the bewildering days and months following, it became clear that military dominance would not be as rapid as first purported. Casualties began to pile up on both sides of the conflict and some began to wonder aloud about the wisdom of the military intervention. Despite the premature televised declaration on May 1st,

2003 of "Mission Accomplished" staged atop the aircraft carrier, *USS Abraham Lincoln*—this was indeed not going to be an easy victory.

Meanwhile, in a far more peaceful place of the planet, a good friend of mine, Salaam, a former captain in the Iraqi Republican Guard during the first Gulf War, had a very unsettled spirit.

He had already been on quite a journey . . .

After Iraq's surrender in 1991 that came about from the united force of a thirty-four nation invasion known as "Operation: Desert Storm", this captain was forced to escape Iraq because of a growing persecution inspired by Saddam Hussein. Due to his ethnic culture of origin, Chaldean, he was considered to be too closely linked with the invading enemy and soon became a prime target for assassination. He and his family were forced to risk life and limb, fleeing Iraq, and eventually making their way to the relative safety of a refugee camp in Athens. There, they hoped and waited for new country, and new home and a new life. One can hardly imagine the excitement this family must have shared when, in 1993, they heard the news that they were permitted to immigrate to Toronto as refugees.

Salaam (which means, 'peace'), had a new start for his family.

Soon after Salaam's arrival to Toronto, he became acquainted with a Syrian church planter who had an unquenchable passion to share the Good News of Christ. This man of God explained to him in his native tongue, Arabic, that coming from a Christian heritage in no way gives you right standing before a holy God. During numerous times of conversation, Salaam was convinced of his need for a Savior and submitted his life to the Lordship of King Jesus.

Salaam, emulating what he had observed in his friend the church planter, soon owned his own passion for sharing the Good News. When I came to know Salaam, he was already leading a congregation of new believers from many nations around the

Middle East. There was no doubt that God had His sovereign hand on his life.

Salaam was deeply troubled about the state of his former nation. In many times and in many ways he asked me to pray for the people of Iraq—a heaviness for his countrymen was very evident in his spirit. As I imagined myself in Salaam's shoes, it was easy to pray. All of his family—brothers and sisters, uncles and aunts, cousins and in-laws were hostage to circumstances beyond their control. Because of this friendship with Salaam, my prayers for Iraq were different than they might have been.

Then, on one perfectly good day, Salaam dropped his own Iraqi bomb.

He looked at me intensely with his deep blue eyes and said, "Jeff, the world is sending soldiers into my country, will the Kingdom of God send any soldiers?"

That was a great question—just as long as Salaam kept things at an abstract-conceptual level. Life is way easier there. But no such luck—Salaam had to get personal. Without blinking, Salaam stared into my soul and asked, "Jeff, will you go with me to Baghdad and encourage the brothers?"

A range of possible responses flashed through my mind—all of them designed to sound somewhat spiritual, but never leading to a scenario that would find me ducking bullets on the crumbling streets of Fallujah. That was not going to happen. The most plausible spiritual-esque sounding reply that came to mind was, "Well, brother, let's pray about that one."

Perfect. He looked convinced.

A few busy days later, I was in a denominational meeting with a dozen other church planters, including Salaam, discussing something that must have been important at the time. The convener appropriately started the meeting with prayer. He asked, "Does anyone have anything heavy on their heart that we can pray together about?" I looked across the circle at Salaam and could see the burden he constantly carried for his homeland. I was the first to volunteer, "We need to pray for Salaam. He asked me to consider going with him to Iraq to help be an encouragement to the pastors under persecution. Pray that we would clearly know God's will in this."

This request, after it was articulated, seemed to have quieted the group. Our convener did something that to me seemed a little unusual: he said, "Alright, let's pray about this. Let's get on our knees and ask the Father to reveal His will in this." Chairs began to be pushed aside and our little band of brothers, kneeling in a circle, began to cry out to God for His clear revelation.

While in the midst of fervent prayer, something quite embarrassing happened—my cell phone, not muted, began to belt out its ringtone. Now I understand the rules of prayer etiquette: first, you never answer the phone when you are in prayer; and second, you never answer the phone when you are in prayer—especially when the people are praying about your prayer particular request. Common sense. But I had an intervening factor that seemed to trump the social conventions of prayer. My house was for sale and my realtor warned me that my first, long awaited offer was about to come in.

God would understand.

I punched the answer button, got up off my knees, and quietly tottered toward the door. Once the door was discreetly shut behind me, I answered in a low voice, "Hello?" The voice on the other end boomed, "Hello Jeff, Bob Roberts here. How are you doing buddy?" "Good," I offered. And then, straight to the point, Bob exclaimed, "Jeff, are you sitting down? I've got an incredible opportunity and I'd like you to join me." He offered two dates, one in May and one in June. "Do you have these open?" "Uh, I don't know, why?" I stammered. Bob explained, "I've got a meeting at the White House and then one at the UN with some very significant people dealing with the complex issues in Iraq. These will be very strategic meetings. Wanna join me?"

Standing in the hallway totally bewildered, I told Bob of the prayer meeting that I had just tiptoed out of. We concluded our discussion with a sense of awe, and then I walked back into the room where my brothers, still on their knees, were praying.

I interrupted their prayer by sharing the story of how God seems to have already answered. We were all in a place of spiritual wonder.

I guess I was going to Iraq.

In the weeks that followed, much preparation was made. Three other courageous volunteers sensed the Lord's leading in joining me: two pastors in our Sanctuary network, Alan Reed and Ron Shepherd, and a friend from South Carolina, Keith Mincey. We felt from the Lord that our assignment was singular: find a leader who was taking spiritual responsibility for his people and see how we can support him. I knew from experience that would-be-leaders were a dime a dozen who would do some great work if people invested in them in advance. We were looking for that unusual leader who was walking by faith to bring the Good News to his people.

The day came to leave the security of Toronto for shelled streets of Baghdad. I wrote notes to my children in case I did not make it home. I kissed my wife goodbye, in a way that seemed far different than any other trip that I had been on. We all realized the stakes of this trip. The Sanctuary had organized prayer covering for us in thirty-minute slots for the two weeks that we would be overseas—and they were taking it seriously—nobody wanted one of their pastors to die on their watch.

Don, a longtime friend of mine, volunteered to drive our group to the airport. He parked his minivan in front of the airport, we unloaded our luggage, and then with a shaky voice, Don stammered, "Guys, could you come back in the van?" We could sense the weightiness in his voice, so we obediently climbed back in. Don pulled a Bible from between the front seats and opened it to about the middle. He said, "I don't know why I am reading this to you pastors, but I think that I am supposed to. It is from Psalm 20:

> *May the Lord answer you in the day of trouble! May the name of the God of Jacob protect you! May he send you help from the sanctuary and give you support from Zion!* (Psalm 20:1-2 ESV)

This seemed a bit strange and comforting all at once. Don was not the kind of friend that would normally lead out in a devotion. Yet, he seemed to be a messenger inspired from the heavenlies. We climbed back out of the minivan with another sense of wonder. When we boarded the plane, we all flopped open our Bibles to Psalm 20 and began to reread that passage. What was the message for us? Our conclusion, although very uncertain, was that God was going to protect us. The 24/7 prayer vigil on our behalf must correlate with, "May he send you help from the sanctuary." To be sure, this passage became a great comfort to us—but none of us was absolutely convinced that this was the whole meaning.

We safely arrived in Baghdad at the height of the insurgency's rebellion and began to witness the destruction of a society. Baghdad was a modern city of eight million people that was organized under a state-directed structure. When someone finished their degree in the university, they became an accountant or teacher or scientist or civil servant in a state sponsored occupation. When the government was destabilized, so also were the majority of jobs. At the time of our visit, the unemployment rate in Baghdad was thought to be as high as sixty percent. Dentists and pharmacists were reduced to standing in front of a building with a machine gun serving as ad hoc security for the smallest measure of financial compensation.

The whole thing was a heartbreaking scene for my Iraqi brother to take in.

Salaam began to leverage his contacts with earnest. Soon we found ourselves in a gathering situated in an upper room of an office complex. About two-dozen pastors from a handful of denominations convened under Salaam's leadership. Salaam began to explain the nature of our mission and asked that the leaders share something of their ministry's vision. These were incredibly inspiring moments as we witnessed the trials of courageous men of God serving Him under the most difficult circumstances imaginable.

Who was the leader we were sent to find? If we didn't find him here, our journey was to take us north to Mosul and then further northwest to Kirkuk before returning to the relative safety of Amman, Jordan.

As these faithful men of God spoke, our hearts were quickened when, a man named Thomas, shared his story. He and his family were ministering in Jordan when the war broke out. While most Christians began to escape Iraq knowing of the hostilities that would soon be directed towards them, Thomas and his family moved back to Baghdad in order to serve King Jesus. He started a church that had two unusual components to its ministry. In the basement, he had a makeshift seminary, where he and two other leaders poured their lives into young men who were preparing to become pastors and church planters. In the attic, he had a series of small windowless rooms that secretly housed young Muslim converts who were preparing for Christian ministry. We were so humbled and inspired by the courageous faith of this leader.

Pastor Thomas invited our group to worship with him on Sunday, and asked if I would preach. We gratefully accepted. But we had no idea what God had in store next.

Sunday came and we made our way back to the building we had visited earlier. It was so obvious that God was moving in this congregation of believers. A building that was designed to accommodate seventy-five people, now somehow managed to hold three hundred. Crowds of Christ followers squeezed themselves into any available square foot that they could find.

We made our way through the tightly packed room and found five white plastic chairs reserved for us on the second row. I opened my Bible and glanced through my notes and asked the Spirit to prepare me to bless and encourage these faithful people. The service started with several worship songs in Arabic with a distinctly Middle-Eastern melody. Then different leaders being trained in the seminary spoke some words—this was truly a wonderful event to witness.

As foreigners not understanding any words being spoken, we heard Arabic, Arabic, Arabic, Arabic, Arabic, Arabic, and then "Psalm 20," and then Arabic, Arabic, Arabic . . . I leaned to my left and asked Alan Reed, "What did you just hear?" He said, "I thought I heard him say 'Psalm 20.'" I leaned forward and asked Pastor Thomas, "What verses in Psalm 20 did he just read?" He said, "The first two."

Two English words amongst thousands of Arabic ones and they were 'Psalm 20.' God had my full attention. I opened my Bible again to those two verses and reread,

> *May the Lord answer you in the day of trouble! May the name of the God of Jacob protect you! May he send you help from the sanctuary and give you support from Zion!* (Psalm 20:1-2 ESV)

The message that I had prepared to preach was now shelved. I had a word of encouragement from our King to share with these precious faithful believers. They were not alone in a struggle against darkness. Jesus was looking after them. He had subjects from another corner of the world who would stand with them. King Jesus was commanding The Sanctuary to send help to this church in the day of their trouble. We would be honored to.

The next day we met with Pastor Thomas and asked him, "How specifically can we help your church?" If I had not already been humbled, he was about to finish the job.

He said, "It's not my church that needs help, God is our help. It is the people of Iraq that need help." He began to explain, "Until now, Iraq has been more of a secular nation than an Islamic one. Christians are not ghettoized like in many other Muslim countries. Our people have lived for years in relative peace with our Muslim neighbors. Now, everyone is afraid. No one has a job. People are hungry. I know that for thirty-five dollars, that we can feed a family of four for a month." He looked at us and said, "Could you help us feed our neighbors in the name of Christ?"

We called Mosul and Kirkuk and offered our apologies for canceling our Monday meetings. We had found the man who was taking spiritual responsibility for his people—the very man of God who the King, in Macedonian-vision-like-style, sent us to find.

We hired a car and set out on our twelve-hour journey speeding across the dry landscape of Iraq to Amman. Crossing the border in Jordan, we breathed a heavy sigh of relief, knowing that we had safely witnessed one of the healthiest expressions of a Kingdom-centered church situated in one of the world's most desperate situations. The Father was humbling all of our hearts.

The five of us checked into a hotel in Amman late that Monday evening and turned on CNN World News eager to find out what had been happening in our corner of the world during the days we were gone. We were not at all prepared to hear the feature story that was being headlined back home.

Earlier that same day, in the late afternoon of Monday, March 16, 2004, on the highway between Mosul and Kirkuk, insurgent combatants surrounded a private passenger car carrying five Baptist missionaries, and opened fire with AK-47 assault weapons. Larry T. Elliott, 60, and Jean Dover Elliott, 58, of Cary, North

Carolina; and Karen Denise Watson, 38, of Bakersfield, California, and David E. McDonnall, 28, of Rowlett, Texas were thought to be dead. His wife, Carrie Taylor McDonnall, 26 had been severely wounded. The group was scouting for a location to build a water purification system.

We sat in our hotel room dazed. We did the math—that was the very road and time that we were scheduled to travel. Why one group of five and not another? Were we more faithful, more significant, or more deserving? Every part of us knew that wasn't so. These missionaries, now wounded and martyred, had given their lives to work in a country that most had already long vacated—these were heroes of the same line as Stephen and James of Zebedee. If it was simply an issue of who was more deserving, we knew that it would have been the other five in the news. There was no way for us to process this. We prayed for the wounded and newly widowed missionary and the families left behind. God continued to break us.

Arriving back to our families and church family in Toronto, we shared the stories of what we had seen and learned. We conveyed the undeniable spiritual obligation that King Jesus had assigned to us. With relative ease one sacrificial gift after another was collected, and tens of thousands of dollars were sent to Pastor Thomas so that he, and his people could feed their hungry neighbors in the name of our King. Soon, Carly, a heroic young lady, would be called out of our church to serve in Baghdad as an instrument for Jesus.

God was teaching us much.

Kingdom Authority

The role of a Kingdom-expanding church becomes tremendously simple—learn to follow the King's instructions, no matter how illogical that they may occasionally sound. If we are ever to see God's hand in our places of ministry, we have no other option but to cooperate with God's ways. Spiritual communities that are designed to advance the name of Christ over and above the notoriety of a well-coiffed brand will be always light the path of faith for Kingdom Seekers to find their home. There is nothing self-seeking in Jesus.

Have you considered how true spiritual authority and a Kingdom-centric design interrelates? Jesus' teaching in Matthew 16 issue a series of questions that Jesus posed that speak with utter clarity to the heart of this issue.

Question number one was the first recorded Christian survey. *What does the world think of Me?* If you were to do a simple thumbs up/thumbs down survey of your neighbors, the results might not be that surprising.

God? Thumbs up.

Jesus? Thumbs up.

Spirituality? Thumbs up.

The Church? Thumbs down.

Those wondering without the hope of a Savior seem to like the product, just not its delivery system. That may be note worthy.

In Matthew 16:13-14, Jesus asked His disciples what the average Israelite thought about him. The consensus seemed to be, "you are the equal to any religious hero we have ever known." Pretty high praise!

That is, if you were not the Son of God.

If we ask our neighbors the same question, we might hear, "He was a prophet, a great teacher, a benevolent and sacrificial religious leader the likes of which the world has never known." Again, high and misguided praise.

Question number two gets a little more personal. *What is the Truth about Me?* Verses 15-17 describe the impetuous Peter shooting up his hand demanding to be the first to answer. In seemingly miraculous fashion, Peter actually gets the answer right: *"You are the Christ, the Son of the Living God,"* he exclaimed. Time well spent with Jesus had led the fisherman to what seemed to be the only obvious conclusion: Jesus was the long awaited Messiah, the one and only hope for redemption, the Agent of Creation come in the flesh.

Score one for Peter.

A third question seems to scream out for an application. *What is the Purpose of this Truth?* This is where things get a little thornier for God's people. There seems to be two answers for the contemporary church. The easy, theological blurt-it-out-without-thinking answer, and the more thoughtful and dangerous way it is practically worked out. In verse 18, Jesus said that Peter's statement of Jesus' supreme Lordship was to be the very foundation of the Kingdom church. It seems to Jesus that the very purpose of the declaration, "Jesus is Lord," was to be the roadmap for how Jesus' church would operate—not merely a theological test of conforming orthodoxy. In short, it would be Jesus' church only when Jesus was literally, practically and completely in charge.

That leads us to question number four. *What is the Power of this Truth?* This fourth question is where the rubber meets the road for the Christian leader. With a decreasing church to population ratio throughout the western world and a downward trending evangelism effectiveness rate in established churches, the question we should all ask is, "where is the power of Lordship of Christ in our land?"

Jesus remarked in verses 18-19, that the power of the church that lived as if Jesus actually was the King would be absolutely unstoppable. Hell's gates would be decimated like Popsicle sticks against the unrelenting onslaught of the obedient people of Light. Darkness' manipulative ways would be no match for wonderful Good News lived and offered freely by the church.

Clearly, as we look at these questions we see a haunting deficit in our land. Like emaciated prisoners of war, our churches too often lack the spiritual fortitude to be a healing agent to its own constituency let alone a preserving force to the communities it claims to serve. Perhaps a final question might help us find our way.

How can we experience the Power of this Truth? How fortunate for us that Jesus gives us a straightforward blueprint in verses 21-25 for a church with a Kingdom-centric design:

1. *We must toss our plans in order to know God's plan.* In verse 21, Jesus explains the normative spiritual process in four disturbing key words, *"go, suffer, be killed, be raised."* These four ideas are repeated throughout Scripture as the keys to power. I first must 'go' and leave my comfort zone. I must 'suffer' by understanding the limits of my flesh. My dependency on human effort must 'be killed' in order to experience God and His 'resurrecting' power.

   Sadly, the seduction of a brand-expanding church growth movement has so influenced the Western church that we now construct plans, one part business, one part religious, that instruct us to behave entirely contrary to Jesus' example. We stay, we don't suffer, we don't die to ourselves, and we never experience the unstoppable life of Christ.

   There is no power or spiritual authority in the 'saving ourselves church.' There is only a delusional short-term fantasy of safety. The reckoning is yet to come.

2. *We must resist the dark temptation of Good Stewardship.* Verses 22-23 describe the fallen human response to the normative spiritual process. In Peter's second bold declaration, "Never Lord!" he scored no points with Jesus. To Peter, good stewardship of the Messiah meant preserve, protect and keep safe. Jesus' plan seemed far too risky. Peter had enough common sense to offer some superior practical advice to this idealistic young 'Messiah.'

   Thud. Jesus was anything but impressed with Peter this time. To Jesus this sentiment of consolidation and good stewardship was not inspired from heaven, but from the very pit of hell. 'Save yourself' sounded far too reminiscent of the hellish counsel issued from a dark tempter. Peter was not as concerned with the Kingdom of God as he was with his own stability, security, and position. The way things were suited him just fine.

The dark doctrine of good stewardship issues its self-serving pearls of wisdom in many ecclesiocentric ways. Some say, "Why should we start new churches? We should be strengthening the ones we have." Translated, "Why should sacred resources be spent on other people when we can still find places to spend them at home?" While in rare cases and in exceptional situations this might be the wisdom of God, typically this sounds much too similar to Peter's dark words. The Kingdom nature of the church of Jesus Christ is to sacrifice ourselves for the sake of a much greater harvest.

So, if consolidation and good stewardship are not the secret to God's strength, what is?

3. *We must cooperate with the spiritual reality of death ushering life.* Again, we find Jesus repeating the pattern of how we experience God's power instead of floundering in our own weakness. In verses 24 we find the instructing terms of, *"come, deny, cross, follow"* which parallel Jesus' earlier self-prophecy of *"go, suffer, be killed, be raised."* It seems that the very limits that the Son of God had put upon Himself as He walked this earth is exactly the life that Jesus asks of His disciples. Jesus caps it off with the revolutionary yet counter-intuitive idea that "saving ourselves" means losing everything and "losing everything" means "finding our life."

Going, suffering, dying, and resurrecting—these are counterintuitive instincts to the primal darkness of self-sufficiency, but are life-giving oxygen to the incapable and dependent in Christ. Jesus' teaching and the chronicles of history show us that miraculous resurrections are exclusively reserved for those who love enough not to love themselves first.

God's power is experienced in our ecclesiastical gatherings only when the King of Kings has authority over His church. This Kingdom-expanding pursuit asks for the full surrender of our weaknesses and insecurities and strengths and advantages to the sole purposes of a singular Sovereign King. Darkness' appeal is to rationalize a more sensible and utilitarian obedience—one that emphasizes good stewardship and our fitting place as master-steward.

Exercising sacred stewardship that is contrary to clearly stated Kingdom intentions would always elicit the same response from heaven as it did when Peter first succumbed to the tempting darkness of his personal preferences:

Get behind me, Satan! You are a hindrance to me. For you are not setting your mind on the things of God, but on the things of man. (Matthew 16:23)

A self-serving hindrance to King Jesus' intentions was never the envisioned design of His church.

SECTION IV

Constructing a Kingdom Design

After the work of deconstructing three widely espoused myths of the modern church, we set about understanding the differences between sources and forms. We have been accustomed to considering the sacred/secular form as a primary distinction, but have observed that it is secondary at best. The greater influence on our behavior is the Source that inspires it. In this, we noted that both the Sources of darkness and the Kingdom of God could profoundly influence the behaviors of both the sacred and the secular.

From these conclusions we constructed a matrix that accounted for both the sources and forms. To discover the effect that sources have on forms, we ran six Kingdom concepts through that matrix: Money, Energy, Change, Community, Love, and Authority.

Now, it is time to put a practical edge to what we have observed. We will do this in two distinct and complementary ways. First, we will look at a series of practical implications that arise from our reflections on the six Kingdom concepts we studied. From these implications, we should have a better picture in mind about the nature of a Kingdom design for a church.

Second, knowing a general picture of Kingdom design, we will look together at a spiritual approach to knowing God's individual design plan for a specific church that advances His Kingdom in the context where He has placed it.

CHAPTER 12

KINGDOM IMPLICATIONS

We have just observed how the very same Kingdom principle appears in such dramatically dissimilar fashions depending on the quadrant of the matrix where it was found. The inspiring Source, and to a lesser degree, the form where it is found, accounts for the wide-ranging variances.

From these observations we can draw six implications that should aid in the design of a church that advances the Kingdom of God.

1. To some, 'attractional' is actually quite unattractive . . .

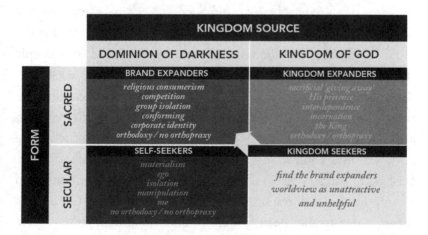

A Grammy's version of church rolled-out slick and easy might be great bait to reel in a self-absorbed self-seeker, but seems to be as enticing to a Kingdom seeker as chitlins and hog-jowls are to the Park Avenue crowd. The whiff emanating from the brand expander's church might be hard to miss, but it is not that compelling. For some, it seems to borders on nauseating.

A church desiring to design a trajectory that would be appealing to a Kingdom seeker should imagine, just for a moment, what it is like to walk in their shoes . . .

Our communities are bustling with a growing sense of volunteerism. Activities that once were limited to a short list of community service clubs now are multiplied tenfold in a myriad of newly birthed volunteer organizations that are filling strip malls, abandoned church buildings and the world wide web. These innovative assemblages have little formal hierarchy, storied traditions, or social prestige—but instead are nimble, focused, and wholly passionate. They are composed of men, women and youth who see the social fault lines in their communities and seem to be internally convicted to be a part of the solution.

The Kingdom seeker, after a long day at work, somehow squeezes in a Wednesday evening once a week, in-between family obligations, to volunteer at a service-dog training center for the blind. Two other members of the family, sensitized by a deeply troubling ordeal that was too close to home, now help with children's programming at a women's shelter. Every weekend in February the whole family joins a posse that seems to mysteriously amass from nowhere, and go door to door throughout the neighborhood on a community food drive for their local food bank. Last year, instead of going to Disney, they decided to volunteer at a camp for the children of their women's shelter. And Christmas, for several years, has been limited to one thoughtful present each, with the extra cash being spent on a backseat full of carefully planned and organized shoeboxes destined for the world's most needy children.

What appeal would spiritual light shows, pink fog, and a sixty-foot cappuccino bar have for this family? What opinion would they have of the socio-spiritual maturity of the church?

And more importantly, would this family expect to find Jesus hanging out there?

Observation shows that Kingdom Seekers find the spiritual worldview of Brand-Expanders as immature and unhelpful.

2. The Kingdom of God has its own gravity . . .

FORM		KINGDOM SOURCE	
		DOMINION OF DARKNESS	KINGDOM OF GOD
	SACRED	BRAND EXPANDERS	KINGDOM EXPANDERS
		religious consumerism *competition* *group isolation* *conforming* *corporate identity* *orthodoxy / no orthopraxy*	*sacrificial 'giving away'* *His presence* *interdependence* *incarnation* *the King* *orthodoxy / orthopraxy*
	SECULAR	SELF-SEEKERS	KINGDOM SEEKERS
		materialism *ego* *isolation* *manipulation* *me* *no orthodoxy / no orthopraxy*	*respond when exposed to the authenticity of the kingdom*

A new church was about to be planted in a city. The pastor of the church planting team, Brett, began by making an appointment with John, a city counselor at city hall. John the counselor was well prepared; he had this meeting many times before. He pre-arranged city-planning maps to show possible worship zoning areas. He boned-up on his bylaw interpretations for religious tax-free exemptions of land use. The answer would be a definitive 'no' when he would eventually be asked for free, or at least greatly discounted city property. He was ready.

Brett brought two paper cups of coffee from the corner coffee shop and handed one to the John. "Here it comes," he thought, "he's already buttering me up." Brett introduced himself and thanked the official for making time for him in his busy schedule. "Sir," Brett said, "I only came here for one reason. You've lived here a long time and understand things that would take me years to learn. I really need your advice."

John was taken aback. This was unlike the beginning of any meeting that he had ever had with a man of the cloth. "Sure," John said with a twinkle in his eye, "always glad to give a preacher a piece of my mind." Brett laughed politely and then looked at the seasoned city counselor straight in his eyes and said, "Sir, we want to make a difference. I believe that a church today should look a lot like Jesus did two thousand years ago. It shouldn't be about what we can get—but about what we can give—what we can do." Brett slowed his pace, "Sir, where are the opportunities in our city that volunteers could touch and make a world of difference? Who is slipping through the cracks that need extra love and attention? What are the social fault lines in our city?"

He wasn't quite as prepared as he thought he was. There was no need for zoning maps and bylaws in this meeting—just an introspective moment to collect his thoughts. "Douglasdale!" he exclaimed. It's filled with single moms and new immigrants and people who need to know that someone cares. There used to be two or three churches there, but they shut down or pulled out. We're starting to get too many reports of crimes in that area. Douglasdale needs what you're talking about."

"Then Douglasdale it is sir," Brett announced. "Once that we're up and working, would you be willing to come and pay us a visit?" Brett asked.

"I wouldn't be a bit surprised son," John said, "We need more clergymen who think like you."

Brett is a good friend of mine. He's one of my heroes. He is a church planter who understands the redemptive and sacrificial nature of the Kingdom-centric church. He, like many others, has rediscovered the gravitational pull that Kingdom activity has upon spirits of Kingdom Seekers. Attacking an injustice head-on seems to inspire the attention and cooperation of those who see the need. The residual wiring that comes from being made in the image of God begins to spark and flicker when exposed to authentic Kingdom living. There is no 'juice' to sustain the life—only spasms and flashes. When the Kingdom seeker observes a spiritual community that sustains a selfless life of sacrificial service—he has many eternal questions to ask . . .

> *But in your hearts set apart Christ as Lord. Always be prepared to give an answer to everyone who asks you to give the reason for the hope that you have. But do this with gentleness and respect.* (1 Peter 3:15 NIV)

Kingdom Seekers respond when exposed to the authenticity of the Kingdom of God.

3. The Kingdom lived creates a compelling draft . . .

The desires of self-seekers and the priorities of Kingdom-expanders are worlds apart. There seems to be very little common ground.

Unfortunately, this does not preclude a self-seeker from entering the sacred arena. A self-seeker may consider being a part of the Brand-Expanders' church—it appeals to many of his self-serving desires. Club memberships in this sacred space offer one benefit after the next. It's a natural fit. The self-seeker spends his remaining days adrift on the *sacred love boat* fulfilling his contractual obligations: he gives his attendance and tithes; he gets whatever he wants. It's perfect. It's like a marriage made in . . .

Well, you know.

How then can an unchurched self-absorbed person connect with a Kingdom-expanding faith community? Usually there is a relational bridge.

Although the bottom left and the top right quadrants seem like they are from different galaxies, they often have a common connection that can become very influential: Kingdom Seekers. This group is often strategically placed as influential liaisons to introduce self-seekers to a whole new idea of life. Here is how we often observe the *draft:*

Neighbors might describe Bob as fun loving, outdoorsy and with a taste for the finer things in life. Terri's description would be far less generous. Piling debt, home maintenance issues too long neglected, and a garage full of top-of-the-line sports equipment has Terri at wits end. And she communicated this often.

Terri has a different dream for life. Coming from a large family, the thought of a mudroom full of tiny tennis shoes has always been close to mind. Big family, big yard, and lots of laughter—that was Terri's dream. But things were not moving forward like she planned. Seven years into their marriage and they have not been able to conceive a child. Bob insisted that a few more visits to the fertility clinic might turn things around but Terri was unconvinced. She was finished, not with her dream, but with the expensive procedures. Life was not turning out as she planned.

Two families in Bob & Terri's neighborhood had children that looked like they represented the UN. Both were part of the same church, and had supported one another as they adopted children from China, the Philippines, Jamaica, El Salvador, and Bosnia. Terri knew these neighbors from a distance, and looked with longing eyes when their children would skip past her house.

She had to talk to these ladies. There were dozens of questions to be answered.

Lois and Cathy were eager to meet with Terri and the neighborhood coffee shop. They curled up on their oversized leather chairs, sipped non-fat lattes and talked global adoption. Terri was astonished to learn that Lois' and Cathy's church had a group of volunteers that helped families navigate the adoption process. In fact, the people of their church had themselves adopted dozens of children from some of the world's most desperate situations. Terri was impressed and had to learn more.

Coffee times were both regular and the highlight of Terri's week. She was inspired by more than Lois' and Cathy's children—she was inspired by their marriages. It was more than that too—it was something about the way they saw life, love, priorities, and faith. Deep things that she carried in her heart for a long time were somehow lived out in Lois and Cathy. What was it?

Two more coffee dates and Terri found the answer. Jesus.

Coffee dates couldn't come fast enough. There was so much to learn. Soon Terri joined a 'small group' that met in Lois' home with six or seven other couples to study the Bible. This small group, or 'coven' as Bob called it, became a lifeline for Terri. In the months that followed, she felt her hostility toward her husband slowly subside. That desperate empty longing for children seem fade as she felt more at peace with herself. Terri indeed was a new creation.

Bob, on the other hand, was not.

His life didn't shape up exactly as he planned either. Once he was the star athlete and the center of attention. Now he spent his time trying to find someone to golf with. And his list of candidates for 'friend' was shorter than he cared to admit. He was lonely and angry and deeply disappointed with life. Now his wife had religion. What else could go wrong?

But all couldn't be bad with Terri's new religion. There seemed to be less huffing and stomping and icy stares since she joined the 'coven.' Buttons that he once pushed to get a reaction now seemed largely ineffective. What's more, Terri asked if he would mind teaching her to golf. She wanted to spend more time with him? Something magical was happening at home. Bob stopped calling Terri's small group a 'coven.'

A few backyard barbeques, movie nights, and adoption meetings later, Bob called Terri's friends his own. For the first time in his life, Bob was ready for an honest conversation about faith.

THE DRAFT

As many have experienced, Bob and Terri's story is typical.

Substitute the names and the story is repeated over and over. The cold, hard reality is that self-seekers share little common ground with Kingdom Expanders, but they are relationally networked Kingdom Seekers. These Kingdom Seekers are pre-packaged with relational equity and credibility to influence self-seekers. When a Kingdom-expanding church is releasing ministry into a community, Kingdom Seekers zone in like homing pigeons. As they enter into relationship with Kingdom focused Christ followers, they recognize that the gravitational pull that they are sensing is directed toward the epicenter of Christ. The transformational effect of a Kingdom-seeker turned Kingdom-expander creates a draft that draws self-seekers into the world of the Kingdom-seeker. From this shift, they are emotionally and spiritually positioned to receive Kingdom light.

The Kingdom lived by the Church of Jesus Christ will serve as a most powerful agent of transformation that a community has ever witnessed. Its impact, written in the stories of people like Bob and Terri, have ripples that emanate through eternity.

4. Self-absorbed churches often contain a few restless, selfless people . . .

KINGDOM SOURCE		
DOMINION OF DARKNESS		**KINGDOM OF GOD**
BRAND EXPANDERS		**KINGDOM EXPANDERS**
SACRED	*will migrate to kingdom building when given an opportunity*	*sacrificial 'giving away' His presence interdependence incarnation the King orthodoxy / orthopraxy*
	SELF-SEEKERS	**KINGDOM SEEKERS**
SECULAR	*materialism ego isolation manipulation me no orthodoxy / no orthopraxy*	*materialism good will isolation manipulation me no orthodoxy / no orthopraxy*

Brand-expanding strategies are designed with high degrees of market precision and are extremely efficient in sucking in everything that isn't nailed down. Like a large commercial combine, everything is blown into the hopper; grain, chaff, weeds, dirt, bugs.

The sorting comes later.

For some, a brand-expanding expression of church is all that they have ever known. The word, 'Kingdom,' is often used, but the ministry spotlight seems pointed indefinitely at the organization's own benefit. Kingdom cooperation with neighboring churches seems to be a soft-minded sentiment; the real message obscurely delivered is, "we will be the king of the hill." Any idea that will cost resources and not deliver a greater market share will never see the light of day.

Many ecclesiocentric pews contain some Christ-followers with a Kingdom-expanding impulse that have little sanctioned opportunity on which to act. Like Joseph of Arimathea or Nicodemus of old, they sneak around under the cover of darkness looking for ways to express this internal motivation, all the while carrying a weird sense of guilt for somehow being disloyal. They passionately love Christ, have created margin in both their time and budget for ministry, but find that all the certified options in the church's catalogue are too sanitized and self-serving.

They need to find a new home.

In starting a new Kingdom-expanding church, or pastoring an existing church that is cultivating a heart for the Kingdom, common wisdom dictates that one must be very cautious in opening the doors of your leadership to transfers from other evangelical churches. The DNA that you are trying to tease out is often very unique. Outsiders storming in with a goods and services version of church can soon stomp the life out of anything that you are fostering. They will soon grow tired of you as well and will hop off to the next show, leaving a trail of carnage behind them.

However, as you ask the Spirit's guidance to sort the wheat from the chaff, you will notice some who have joined your community with wonderful motivations. They hadn't left a previous situation disgruntled. They don't have bad things to report about your 'competitors.' They were simply attracted to your fellowship because of what they had observed you doing in the community.

A lesser draft can find Kingdom Expanders in a Brand-Expander's edifice and draw them home from top left quadrant to top right.

Keep your eyes open for these rare saints.

5. Kingdom expansion normally comes without loud accolades . . .

KINGDOM SOURCE		
	DOMINION OF DARKNESS	**KINGDOM OF GOD**
SACRED	BRAND EXPANDERS *religious consumerism* *competition* *group isolation* *conforming* *corporate identity* *orthodoxy / no orthopraxy*	KINGDOM EXPANDERS *require a resolute resistance* *to the temptations of brand* *expanders for the sake* *of the kingdom*
SECULAR	SELF-SEEKERS *materialism* *ego* *isolation* *manipulation* *me* *no orthodoxy / no orthopraxy*	KINGDOM SEEKERS *materialism* *good will* *isolation* *manipulation* *me* *no orthodoxy / no orthopraxy*

(Left axis: **FORM**)

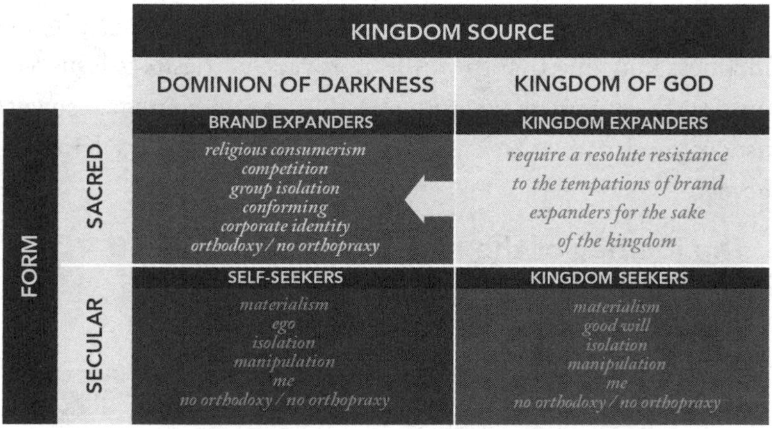

Nickels and noses, buildings and budgets; this is the currency of the Brand-Expander. However, not all churches with high currency are motivated so basely. Many leverage their success into astonishing Kingdom gains. These churches inspire many Kingdom leaders to sacrificial ministry that will result in multiplication. But even with this focus, sometime smaller churches miss the Kingdom nuances and simply strive to emulate the exteriors of a larger Kingdom-focused church with predictably disappointing results. Kingdom-expansion is never one more program to be added to a self-serving list.

Unfortunately, the scorecard that seems to be almost exclusively employed to receive 'atta boys' from Christendom's machinery appears to be far too closely linked to the currency of the Brand-Expander. Kingdom expansion normally comes without loud accolades. I wonder if that is why Jesus repeated the promise that Kingdom investors will receive the most sincere of all accolades directly from His own lips:

Well done, good and faithful servant. You have been faithful over a little; I will set you over much. Enter into the joy of your master. (Matthew 25:23 ESV)

Kingdom-expanding leaders most often endure obscurity and loneliness knowing that the only approval they desire is Jesus' very own. To these leaders we ask God to give you courage, tenacity, wisdom, and patience as you sow eternal seeds for a Kingdom harvest.

6. The journey of the Kingdom Seeker is a destination to the King.

KINGDOM SOURCE		
	DOMINION OF DARKNESS	**KINGDOM OF GOD**
SACRED (FORM)	**BRAND EXPANDERS** *religious consumerism* *competition* *group isolation* *conforming* *corporate identity* *orthodoxy / no orthopraxy*	**KINGDOM EXPANDERS** *sacrificial 'giving away'* *His presence* *interdependence* *incarnation* *the King* *orthodoxy orthopraxy*
SECULAR	**SELF-SEEKERS** *materialism* *ego* *isolation* *manipulation* *me* *no orthodoxy / no orthopraxy*	**KINGDOM SEEKERS** *find fulfillment in their quest* *only when they discover the* *authority of 'the King'*

A Kingdom-seeker can only find fulfillment in his life's quest when he discovers and trusts the saving authority of the King. This journey of a Kingdom-seeker is simply a destination to the King. The spiritual signals he receives are beacons from heaven sounding the course to the King. If he is going to find the King, the King's subjects had better organize their priorities around what Kingdom Seekers instinctively know to be true. In that way we will prove that we are 'people of the Book.' And maybe a better handle: we might prove that we are 'His disciples.'

If we, the church, are not about the King's business, how will today's desperate multitudes of Kingdom Seekers ever find their way to Him?

Let me close this book with one final story.

I had the privilege of being in a small group of pastors who were talking with a hero of the faith. Probably very few who are reading this will have ever heard of him. He started and is pastoring a house church network in Vietnam that numbers in the thousands. In the midst of intense persecution and scant resources, this man of God had tenaciously persisted in his faithfulness to Jesus. His appearance was humble—his testimony was powerful.

Two of my fellow pastors began to ask this spiritual giant a series of leading questions seeking to understand his system of doctrinal orthodoxy. The enquiries finally led to the blunt question, "You have all these house churches scattered around your region, what curriculum or process do you use to ensure that your leaders are teaching sound doctrine?"

The gentle Vietnamese pastor had patiently been answering all the preceding questions. When the final one was launched, he seemed a little confused; he thought that he had already answered it several times. He took a deep breath, and began to speak in his broken English:

"This is how we teach our leaders. We open our Bibles. We read a verse. We ask our people if they are doing that verse. If not, we do not go on to the next verse. That is how our leaders do our Bible."

And this is the life of a Kingdom Expander.

And this is the hope of a Kingdom-seeker.

CHAPTER 13

KINGDOM DESIGN

And so we have taken quite a journey.

We started out by deconstructing some popular Christian myths related to the Kingdom of God by looking at the biblical evidence. We analyzed the myth of a third kingdom and concluded that it did not exist. At any moment I am building either the Kingdom of God, or the dominion of darkness. My actions are inspired by one of two spiritual sources. There is no mushy middle.

We looked at the myth of church growth and rediscovered that all that is done in the name of church advancement does not necessarily advance the Kingdom of God. And if there is no middle kingdom, then the actions of some church advancing strategies actually decrease God's Kingdom.

The final myth we examined was the myth of Kingdom turf. Here we discovered that those who claim stewardship of the sacred form do not hold the property rights of the Kingdom. There are Kingdom Seekers who hold in high esteem the values of our King. They are on a journey that can easily end in meeting the Kingdom's Source.

After an exercise in myth deconstruction, we set about trying to make sense of what we understand and observe. We concluded that the sacred/secular division of forms is limited in importance when compared to the utterly influential sources that inspire our behavior.

Our reconstruction of forms and sources gave expression to four very different categories of behavior: the self-seeker, the Brand-Expander, the Kingdom-seeker, and the Kingdom-expander. Each quadrant occupied an easily understood form while being inspired by a lesser-understood spiritual source.

Upon reconstruction, we took a peek at what several significant Kingdom principles looked like in each quadrant of the matrix. We examined money, energy, change, community, love, and authority noticing radically different worldviews that aligned more closely to the sources that inspired them than the forms that they occupied.

We concluded our observations by gathering six conclusions of how people tend to move through the matrix. It became acutely apparent that much hinges on the success of the church of Jesus Christ occupying the territory of the Kingdom Expander.

Now what?

With all that we have discovered, it becomes obvious that the Christian leader must have a clear understanding of the Kingdom assignment in which the King is asking him to lead. Without it, we are once again wandering in the wilderness with slightly upgraded tabernacles.

But how does a Kingdom leader accurately understand his Kingdom assignment? There are clues. Let me share another story.

I was asked to fly to South America and share with a group of missionaries about what we had learned in our church planting work in Toronto. Specifically, I was asked to help this team to gain a vision and strategy for their shared work. The meeting was to be held in a retreat setting in an extremely isolated area high in the Andes Mountains.

I had thought through some general ideas of what I would share, but had nothing as solid as I would like. On the fourteen-hour plane ride, I asked God to give me something that would

encourage these selfless leaders and perhaps help them discover His plan for their corner of the globe.

As I quieted my heart, God began to remind me of how He had directed my steps over the past years. With scratch pad and pen in hand, I began to jot down the process that He brought to my mind. It became a simple algebraic formula. It expressed precisely the patterns that I had seen and learned from many faithful leaders who have gone before me.

The time together seemed to encourage my missionary friends—for that I was grateful. I have used this little idea numerous times to help church planters construct a strategy that could have a Kingdom punch. It is exciting to watch a leader replace a strategy pirated from another context with one spoken directly to his heart from the familiar voice of his King.

Perhaps it might help you.

How to design a church for the Kingdom of God:

$$\underset{\text{VISION}}{\overset{\text{GOD'S}}{\text{KINGDOM}}} = [\overset{who}{\text{SG}} + \overset{where}{\text{PE}} + \overset{whose}{\text{PA}}\ (\text{Context}^{3}*)]\ \text{A.S.P.}$$

* micro intel
macro intel
repro intel

GOD'S KINGDOM VISION

If the church is going to occupy the land of the Kingdom-expander, it follows that it will have to design its strategies in submission to will of the One who sees from a much higher vantage. With the faith to believe that God's ways are higher than our ways, we set an open course allowing the King to direct the sails.

This process involves three areas of discovery. First I must know who I am. Second, I must understand where I am. Finally, I must re-establish Whose I am. This simple exercise of humility, understanding and surrender can guide a spiritual leader to a powerful Kingdom-expanding design for life and ministry.

		KINGDOM SOURCE	
		DOMINION OF DARKNESS	KINGDOM OF GOD
FORM	SACRED	BRAND EXPANDERS	KINGDOM EXPANDERS
			GODS KINGDOM VISION = [SG+PE+PA (Context^{i*})] A.S.P. *micro intel* *macro intel* *repro intel*
	SECULAR	SELF-SEEKERS	KINGDOM SEEKERS

Know <u>who</u> you are: SG + Pe + Pa

The first problem with borrowing a successful blueprint from somewhere else is that it originated from the heart and life experiences of another leader. God spoke to him or her. The design was specific to the spiritual gifts, personality and passions of that leader. The very reason that it might be 'borrow-worthy' is that it expressed the King's desires for another place and time.

The good news is that our Father has perfect plans for each of his children. The design will start with an accurate accounting of our gifts, personalities and Divinely inspired passions.

If you are a church planter, this assignment is relatively simple. You will start by looking honestly at your past, and from that observation, perceiving the possible trajectory of your future. The future DNA of your new church will take its cues from this exercise.

If you are in leadership of an established church, the task is slightly more complex. Instead of individual analysis, you have the have the need to perform a more corporate analysis—looking at the overall trends and themes of how God has shaped the congregation. However, even in an existing church setting, it is vital that the senior pastor go through this process as distinct from the congregational snapshots. God has appointed this leader as under-shepherd and likely has something to say through his personal makeup.

If you are in neither of the two previous categories, but are in the process of investigating to discover your place in the Kingdom, your approach will differ slightly. You might not yet have a long track record of observations from which to draw conclusions. Your approach will require spiritual sensitivity to the impressions that you have been sensing about future steps of faith. This will likely be significant to your future Kingdom design.

SG: Spiritual Gifts

The most significant level of self-discovery is getting a clear picture of how much we have changed since becoming a subject of the King. The day we submitted our lives to the Lordship of Christ we received His Spirit as an indwelling and ever present guide. This indwelling Spirit sensitizes us to the King's desires. Through a relationship of humble submission guided by the authority of His living Word we begin to sense God's plan.

This plan will often involve two uncomfortable steps that force us to reflect on our insecurities and weigh them against the omnipotence of God: First, it will highlight areas of our personal weakness. We sense that God is leading us toward something that isn't requiring our greatest personal assets. Our standard *modus operandi* of leading with our strengths is asked to take a backseat along with our pride.

This leads us to the second awkward step. Having a good grasp on our weaknesses, God often leads us to make faith steps that center on those fragilities. In faith, with the full awareness of my shortcomings, I obediently take steps toward the impossible assignment of God. In this weakness, we begin to discover our spiritual gifts. With them, we discover the strength of our King.

Stuttering shepherds often become the greatest Kingdom leaders.

This understanding might sound radically different than the understanding you might have gained through previous exercises with spiritual gift inventories. Gift inventories most often focus on our aptitudes, abilities, and preferences. Questions like, "in situation A would you most likely 1, 2, or 3?" Our answer more aptly describes the strength of our personality than an opportunity to see God's strength immerge through that personality. Thus, after completing our two hundred questions, we have taken a completely accurate sacred personality test rather than discovering anything truly spiritual. The sacred personality test is not unimportant, but equating its calculated deductions with a spiritual gift may rob us of the opportunity of discovering God's greatest blessing in our ministries.

Instead of looking inward to our strengths in search for clues of a spiritual gift, it would be wiser to look backward to our past. Look at the sweeping themes of our personal histories; pay careful attention to the times where steps of faith have been taken and where God has shown up in remarkable ways. What was the greatest faith issue? What personal weakness caused the greatest internal struggle? What were the lessons learned from those experiences? The answers to questions like these may well lead to the identification of the Spirit's gifting of our lives. Our weakness, God's empowering strength—a truly spiritual gift.

The design of a Kingdom-expanding ministry will always account for the King's powerful presence working His will through our yielded weakness.

Pe: Personality

We have dismissed the sacred personality test as non-instructive to the discovery of spiritual gifts, however, this does not mean that the Kingdom design of our ministries is unrelated to our unique personalities. God has given our personalities as a gift in which to glorify Him. These varied personalities reflect something of the nature of God as it is expressed through people.

Our personalities are the 'hard-wiring' of how we approach the world. This individual personality becomes the lens by which we take in information and formulate a response. Varied people will approach the same situation and deduce considerably different courses of action largely propelled by the filter of their personalities. The Kingdom design of any ministry will show God's fingerprints by accounting for the personality He has created us with.

Personalities are varied. Some of us are energized in being with people; others need to draw alone to recharge our batteries. Some of us are sensible, down to earth people who make practical choices for efficiency and effectiveness. Others of us are highly imaginative and creative, with abilities to intuitively discover new paradigms and processes. Some of us are very focused people; we know what we want to accomplish and cannot rest until the list has been completed. Others are much more free-flowing in accomplishing assignments—new information does not derail our plans, but simply redirects them. Some of us are logical and systematic in how we approach a problem and are not deeply affected by the emotions around us. Others of us take our cues from the sentiment of the situation and respond as the circumstances dictates.

Varied personalities, each fashioned by God and a strategic part of His Kingdom's design. Knowing and appreciating the unique personality that God has given us will serve us well in understanding our place in God's Kingdom-expanding plans.

Pa: Passions

Passions are the deep places where God lights up His Kingdom priorities in our spirit. They are unique to us as individuals and often originate from past experiences in which we have been profoundly touched. These experiences compel us toward a particular problem or cause with little need for stimulus of an outside motivation. Passions often have a life of their own.

But passions by nature are not the exclusive territory of the Kingdom of God. As we observed earlier, dark passions can often become self-serving obsessions in the sacred space. For passions to be Kingdomcentric, they will direct the objects of that passion to the healing, comfort and transforming authority found in our King, and in turn be strategically released to guide others to their newfound Source of life.

Understanding our Kingdom passions becomes essential in designing a church for the Kingdom of God. Through an acute awareness of our Kingdom passions, our ministries gain focus and motivation that a mere reproduction of a ministry model could never inspire. Passions guide and propel.

Knowing who I am is necessary to understanding how God might desire to use me in His Kingdom-expanding plans. God's Kingdom design for my life will account for my weakness and His strength (spiritual gifts), my unique hard wiring (personality), and the internal Kingdom motivators that direct my actions (passions). Understanding these three will be the first step in developing a Kingdom design.

Know <u>where</u> you are: Context[3]

After getting a firm grip on reality as to the nature of who we really are, we are prepared for the next step. Now we perform the task of analyzing the spiritual, emotional and intellectual soil of the geography that God has assigned us. A Kingdom-expanding design will, by nature, have an impulse that emanates out and convincingly introduces a lost and dying world to the hope of Christ.

Spiritual reconnaissance is necessary in order to establish a Kingdom design for the church that actually connects with the spiritual issues and objections of Kingdom Seekers.

There are three contextual spheres in which to investigate and from that analysis, build meaningful strategies. The three spheres of context are: Micro-intelligence, which answers the question, "In our context, what is the process that a Kingdom-seeker finds his way to the King?" The second is macro-intelligence, which tries to ascertain, "In our context, how would groups of King-dom-seekers most likely find their way into the Kingdom of God?" And finally, reproductive-intelligence, which answers, "If this is truly a Kingdom design, what contextual systems of repro-duction might be developed in order to release God's people for Kingdom-expansion?"

We will look very briefly at these three dimensions of con-text. Our careful reconnaissance will serve us well in designing a church for the Kingdom of God.

Micro-Intelligence

At this point we are trying to discover the normative way that a Kingdom-seeker in a particular context of culture finds his way to the King. In contexts that have had the benefit of much positive Gospel seed sowing, it might be a fairly direct line between the pre-Christian and his or her confession of faith in Christ. Unfor-tunately, those areas seem to be increasingly rare.

If the context of culture has not had the advantage of soaking in a positive Christian environment, the Kingdom-seeker's journey to Christ, most often, becomes a series of mini-decisions. These mini-decisions are the responses that a pre-Christian makes in overcoming personal objections on the road to salvation. The typical hurdles that this person encounters relates to his heart, his mind, and finally his spirit. Usually in that order.

First objection: The Heart. If a non-believer has had a negative experience with a professing Christian of a church, there is generally an emotional roadblock that prevents him from being open to the Gospel. This emotional barrier, from the perspective of the Kingdom-seeker, is generally much taller and wider than any picture of Christ that can be painted with a harvesting-intended Gospel presentation. If a lost person's negative experiences lead him to the sincere conclusion that Christians are hypocrites, than a harvesting approach will most often be offensive and unproductive.

This is the stage of cultivation.

In this stage, a Kingdom-expanding Christ-follower, by the character of his faith and testimony, can demonstrate an authentic devotion in action. This is very powerful stuff. God can take one faithful witness and overpower years of scorched earth brought about by sacred people with dark behaviors.

The stage of cultivation is the work of the witness empowered by the Holy Spirit.

Second objection: The Mind. If the Kingdom-seeker has intellectual difficulties with the tenets of the Gospel, no slick harvesting techniques can induce a genuine and wholehearted commitment to Christ. If, as discussed earlier, a person believes that Christianity is no better or worse than any other religion—if there is a God, then all roads must lead to Him—then calling for a decision is premature. His questions need real answers. And fortunately for us, the Word of God is cover to cover with real answers.

This is the stage of sowing.

In this stage, the Kingdom-seeker must, in relationship, hear and understand an alternate reality to his long held intellectual difficulties. A patient, gentle and careful explanation of the Gospel and its implications will chip away at this barrier, until one day, the seeker realizes that he no longer holds his former ideas.

The stage of sowing is the work of the Word empowered by the Holy Spirit.

Third Objection: The Spirit. With the leveling of both *heart* and *mind* barriers, the Kingdom-seeker is emotionally and intellectually prepared to genuinely respond to the Gospel's invitation with a whole and sincere heart. The lone barrier that stands is one of volition. The questions of reaping are now entirely appropriate.

This is the stage of harvesting.

In this stage, the witness acts much like a midwife in this new birth of the Holy Spirit. The Kingdom-seeker has been on a journey that has overcome objections that had distanced his heart from the message of Christ. In becoming open to the messenger, he has become open to the message. He has laid down intellectual challenges and instead picked up clear biblical teachings that have relieved his restless mind. For the first time in his life, because of the patience of the witness, the Kingdom-seeker can see a true picture of Christ's love. He is ready to respond.

The stage of harvesting is the work of the Holy Spirit midwifed by the witness.

And so we see that micro-intelligence helps us understands the typical process a Kingdom-seeker in a given context of culture makes his way to the cross of Christ. For some contexts, this is a shorter trip than in others.

This information will be invaluable for the next step.

Macro-Intelligence

If micro-intelligence aids us in understanding how an individual in a context of culture typically responds to Christ—macro-intelligence seeks to help us ascertain how groups of people may travel down that road. This reconnaissance becomes particularly strategic when designing a church for a Kingdom-expanding assignment because understanding where major portions of its population are 'stuck' will speak strongly on how to proceed.

Macro-intelligence gathers critical information to devise a tactical plan of operation. Again, the spiritual history of the landscape you are operating within will inform the church on pressure points that will need extra spiritual attention. For instance:

If the culture of context has been over-seeded with negative exposure to Christianity, the *heart* objections are generally high. Strategies that aim at the mind or the spiritual resolve will usually be ineffective. The population's emotional barriers to the Gospel need to be leveled first. Employing the ideas of micro-intelligence, on a corporate scale, will help a population group receive a different image of Christ and His followers.

In this stage, a Kingdom-expanding church can cultivate its field of context by addressing a generally understood social fault line within its community. The selfless living out the implications of the Gospel by lovingly addressing a broken point in a community will drastically reposition the future effectiveness of the church. By engaging Kingdom Seekers in the process, the evangelism process speeds up and an emotionally healthy leadership base is developed for further ministry.

If macro-intelligence points to little negative exposure to Christianity, but significant intellectual objections—our strategies need to adjust. The contexts of culture where *mind* barriers are highest are usually found in very secularized environments. Here, there has been little contact with the Gospel allowing multiple generations to ingrain and personalize the doctrines of secularization. This group is often incongruently both altruistically idealistic and sordidly practical. A two-pronged approach can be effective.

In their practical pursuits, standards have been lowered from the morality of 'right and wrong' to a shorter-term perspective of 'what works.' By alternating teaching themes between the practical benefits of living God's truth to straightforwardly addressing intellectual objections from a biblical worldview, many Kingdom Seekers will find an appeal. In highly secularized environments, people are not accustomed to authoritative teaching; when combined with a transparent humility, the Kingdom-seeker often becomes spiritually intrigued. An open door for Gospel sowing is swung wide.

To address altruistic idealism, the Kingdom-expanding church needs to create significant distance between their own positioning within the community and the notion that 'church' brings to many Kingdom Seekers. To many in this space, a brand-expanding self-serving collection of superficial saints is the disreputable image that 'church' connotes. By working hand in hand to address neglected social needs in a community, the Kingdom-seeker not only gets to sense the repercussions of the Gospel, but also is placed in relationship with Christ-followers to understand its Source. New ideas for 'Christianity' and for 'church' are formed in his mind. Ideas that deeply impress him.

If macro-intelligence suggests that neither the barriers of the *heart*, or the *mind* exist, a straightforward harvesting approach would be appropriate. However, this context might be difficult to find.

Reproductive-Intelligence

And so a thorough reconnaissance of the context of culture has taken place with helpful discoveries for the best path that both individuals and groups travel toward the King. Now we are at the point of designing a multiplying plan for major Kingdom advancement.

Reproductive-intelligence considers both micro and macro-intelligence, and within that framework, seeks to develop contextual systems of Kingdom-expanding reproduction as the primary outcome. To discuss this concept at any depth would be a book on its own. Instead we will limit our discussion to the basic demarcations of a Kingdom design.

Before we can effectively consider this, we must first have clear thinking on what we consider to be a healthy Kingdom design. Much discussion over the past years on the subject of church health has primarily centered on internal functions within the church. Keying on Jesus' teaching on the primacy of Kingdom fruit as basic indicator of life, perhaps a dedicated outcomes oriented scorecard would more accurately measure a church's Kingdom vitality.

Four marks of a Kingdomcentric church[¶]:

Vital signs are significant to a physician in quickly ascertaining the general health of a patient. Vital signs are not a comprehensive picture of a person's health, but if something is awry in any one of them, major health complications usually follow. In the same way, the following four marks of a Kingdomcentric church do not describe every nuance of health, but the gaps tell a troubling story of design.

1. New Believers

If a community of faith grows at a fast pace, but baptisms are limited to children from already believing families growing in their own commitment to Christ, and the previously evangelized transferring in and submitting to a new mode of baptism—would this be a healthy church? Certainly any measurements of health

---

[¶]I am grateful for the visionary leadership of Gerry Taillon, E.D. of Canadian National Baptist Convention (CNBC). Gerry has led the CNBC to fashion and adopt these four vital signs as the primary structuring of his team.

should look to see if new believers are being regularly added to the family of faith.

Reproductive-intelligence would account for a systemic design that would effectively implement the discoveries made in macro-intelligence.

2. New Disciple-makers

If disciple-making, that is helping the evangelized to become fishers of men themselves, is not a part of a church's strategic processes—is it obeying the commission of Christ? A Kingdomcentric church defines this understanding of the disciple early on in the discipleship process.

Reproductive-intelligence will design training and accountability processes that sync with its micro-intelligence to boost the evangelistic efficiency of the church. Pastors and worship services become support structures for a membership that understands its Kingdom assignment.

3. New Communities of Faith

Any definition of church health that does not account for the normative reproduction of its Kingdom assignment in other geographies and cultural expressions should be dismissed as a relic of a more self-serving era. A church with no plans or strategy in place to 'give itself away' to populations and geographies with little or no access to an effective Gospel proclaiming church cannot consider itself whole.

Reproductive-intelligence will design a roadmap for a Kingdom-expanding church to sacrificially plant, or partner in planting, new congregations as a normal part of its lifestyle. Macro-intelligence will reveal gaps, whether they are affinity-based, linguistic, or cultural, that is underserved with the Gospel.

4. Transforming Communities

Finally, as we have already discussed at length, is it possible to consider a church to be healthy that has little or no transformative presence in the community in which it exists? Certainly Christ's notion of His unstoppable community would more closely resemble His own personal ministry than our best ideas on a well-polished worship experience.

Reproductive-intelligence advises a Kingdomcentric church how to release its membership as selfless agents of transformation wherever they exist. The testimony of this health indicator can be observed as salt and light penetrating hidden places that a sacred service could never find.

Four distinct Kingdom characteristics, reproducing by nature, that express our King's charge to His people. The church of Jesus Christ, united together and dreaming the very desires of the King Himself is an amazing thought to behold.

Designing a church for the Kingdom of God will always be reminiscent of a heroic mission for one very loved and lost lamb.

Know <u>Whose</u> you are: ASP—*Absolute Surrender in Prayer*

And now the rubber hits the road.

We have spent time in honest reflection discovering the uniqueness of our fascinating and complex selves. God's creative investment in each of us demands far more than a less than perfect reproduction of someone else's life mission. God has something to say about His desires through our very weaknesses and His strength manifested through our lives in a truly spiritual gift. His fingerprints on our very personality give hint to a Kingdom design. Couple these with a unique passion that we cannot shake off—and we begin to see a picture of the kind of Kingdom leader that God is asking us to become.

There is no one quite like you.

And then we have thought carefully about what it might be like to be a Kingdom-seeker in the contexts where we live. We have imagined the possible barriers that block him from gaining a clear view of Jesus. We have pulled the lens back from that tight focus and tried to imagine a ministry design that would become a clearly marked path for groups of Kingdom Seekers in our varied contexts to travel to Jesus. More than likely our paradigms of church are being stretched. Taking all this contextual information into account, we dreamed together about what a church that majored on the Kingdom idea of reproduction might look like. Systems well-designed to produce a steady flow of Kingdomcentric results measured in new believers, new disciple-makers, new communities of faith and a transforming effect on our communities. We begin to see that this will not be a church design copied from a conference.

Likely, there will be no church quite like yours. Or should I say, 'His.'

And this takes us to our third and final exercise. Absolute surrender in prayer. We lay down everything that we know about ourselves and everything that we know about our contexts—and declare our exclusive allegiance to the King of the Kingdom . . .

"Your Kingdom come,
Your will be done
through
and in
me."